TRANSFORMATIONAL
Job Strategies

For Getting the Job You Want

By Lawrence Frederick Peterson Ph.D.

Copyright 2012 Lawrence Peterson

TABLE OF CONTENTS

Introduction

WORKING SMARTER NOT HARDER

THE INFORMATION AGE

MARKETING PSYCHOLOGY

CORPORATE MISSIONS MAKE FOR BETTER INTERVIEWS

REVERSE PSYCHOLOGY

INNOVATORS VERSUS MAINTAINERS

NO SUCH THING AS EXACT QUALIFICATIONS

COMPENSATION IS RELATED TO NEEDS

INTERVIEWS ARE 99% PSYCHOLOGICAL

RUNNING THE CAREER SERVICE MAZE

THE HIDDEN JOB MARKET

FINDING THE RIGHT WORK ENVIRONMENT

ONE OUT OF MANY

RESUME EXAMPLES

INTERVIEW QUESTIONS AND ANSWERS

PSYCHOLOGICAL CRABS

30 DAYS TO A MORE SUCCESSFUL CAREER

HOW TO FIND INFORMATION ABOUT COMPANIES

INTRODUCTION

When you know what the magician knows, your job search becomes magically transformed. Whether employed and looking for a better opportunity or temporarily unemployed and needing immediate work, the career maze has suddenly been road mapped and simplified. The psycho-strategies explained in this handbook stem from countless interviews with clients, business leaders and personnel specialists. The strategies will work for anyone who applies them. Read this handbook and commit the principles to memory. Clients applying the principles contained herein have established meaningful careers and so will you.

Psychology teaches us we are motivated by self-interest more than altruism. Companies are no different. Learning to identify and align your self-interest to the interest of the company affords the best opportunity for career growth. Differences between individual and company expectations can thwart opportunities for compensation and occupational fulfillment. Finding and exploiting the right job fit is the focus of this handbook.

Changes in technology are causing upheaval in the workplace. Keeping the same job until retirement is no longer a realistic expectation. Where traditionally manufacturing employed a large segment of the workforce, the service industry and the cubical office now represent a lion share of job openings in the modern era. Full time is being replaced by flex time and home based jobs are becoming more commonplace for jobs in sales, marketing, customer service and on-line educational training.

Mergers, corporate takeovers, leveraged buyouts and restructuring are displacing a growing number of workers. Being between jobs is a certainty at one time or another. Forecasts suggest the average worker will occupy no less than fifteen jobs in his or her career. Learning the secret to job marketing has never been more crucial. New career opportunities are continually surfacing. Opportunities look promising in cancer genomics, synthetic cells, chromosome separation, robotics, solid-state batteries, energy conservation, social indexing, crash proof code, gesture interface, data encryption, and cloud streaming. Job candidates will find success in pursuing work associated with biomedicine, network systems analysis, personal and home care aide, finance, medical science, and internet marketing. Even if there are not enough jobs to go around, there are always jobs to be had.

An interesting experiment was performed where a group of candidates were asked to complete a test while surrounded by construction noise. A second group of candidates was give the option of pressing a button to reduce the noise if it became too distracting. Although candidates in the second group never elected to press the button, they scored better than the first group because they perceived they had control over the distracting noise. Better jobs and happier lives are possible by learning to take control our job destinies. By incorporating into your search strategy the proven fundamentals found in this handbook you will no longer fear finding a new position.

Companies have long known humans are not completely practical and are using neuromarketing to persuade customers to purchase goods and services by applying the principles of psychology to sale and marketing programs. The same principles of persuasion can be applied to your job seeking process with similar results. Employers take less than five minutes to unconsciously decide if they are going to hire a job candidate. If you do not understand the simplicity and predictability of how to make a positive impression, a lot of job offers will be lost. Job candidates from diverse backgrounds, education levels, and career experience are afforded a glimpse behind the veil of the Wizard of Jobs. One glimpse and your job search strategies will be forever changed.

WORKING SMARTER NOT HARDER

Working smart and working hard are two different animals.

OLD STYLE APPROACHES TO WORK

Work dissatisfaction is the single most recurring complaint among workers today. This observation is supported by occupational statistics suggesting over eighty percent of all employees are working well below skill level. Mundane, perfunctory job descriptions encourage boredom, fatigue and migraine headaches. All organisms have an inherent tendency to actualize their potentialities. Feeling trapped in a dead end job reduces motivation and productivity. Though job stress is becoming increasingly commonplace, the threat of unemployment is linked to free floating anxiety, high blood pressure and chronic fatigue syndrome. Stress and job dissatisfaction is elevated through workplace politics, micromanaging, sudden salary cuts, changes in benefits, and pressure to complete tasks within unrealistic timelines. The Economy Policy Institute suggests worker dissatisfaction stems from income not keeping pace with inflation rates. Though progressive companies are offering programs to help employees exercise, lose weight and control stress, competition, potential cutbacks, restructuring and hostile takeovers encourage a wide range of anxieties. Despite New Age industries offering employees biofeedback and meditation breaks for stress, millions of dollars are still spent each year for prescription medication to fight tension and depression due to the ravages of work. Reasons for finding a rewarding job with commensurate compensation have never been more important to mental health.

The Center for Disease Control states forty-percent of workers report their job as extremely stressful and a quarter of employees view their job as the number one stress producer in their lives. Similarly, the Bureau of Labor Statistics report approximately forty million workers are experiencing severe stress at work with no quick fix available. Programs are being developed to recognize and prevent burnout, reduce workplace conflict and how to manage crisis. Since necessity is considered the mother of invention the solution to alleviating stress associated with a toxic job or career is to change jobs, change companies or change careers. The old style approach to changing jobs was to wait until you were terminated. Proactive job candidates look for opportunities for a better career fit. Learning how to strategically change is fundamental to developing your job hunting skills.

YOU ARE WHAT YOU DO FOR A LIVING

The growth in national healthcare expenditures is well above the inflation rate and we now spend billions per year to provide health benefits for the general population attributable to employment related circumstances. When we realize the single most important determinant of social rank and prestige is what people do for a living, it is easy to extrapolate from the data problems with health are directly and indirectly connected to occupational status. Work has become an institutionalized projection of the Self. You are what you do for a living. Once you appreciate this insight, you see why unemployment, under-employment, and being passed over for a promotion are viewed as the ultimate pariah. Understanding your basic personality style can minimize stress associated with poor job fit. Where some job candidates would be happier in line management positions, other job candidates would find solace in staff support positions. A common by-product of poor job fit is stress which undermines our mental and physical health. Fortunately, this handbook seeks to provide the reader with greater control of their career destiny for improved health and compensation.

Two sociologists performed an experiment where they started work in a factory to gauge the influence of the company on their professional behavior. In a very short time period, both admitted to cheating on production numbers because it was expected in their department. Jobs can be a blessing or our worst nightmare.

Another interesting study showed an increase in testosterone in workers assuming positions of higher authority. Our surroundings and job description directly affect our hormone secretion, which in turn, impact on our behavior.

An extension of this research suggests when we act as if we already have the job, we convey those attributes generally associated with the position. When our behavior is consistent with the job, employers are more likely to respond with congruence and job offers.

Anticipating job opportunities is an important part of career development. The future is not likely to compliment manufacturing and farming. Peter Drucker suggested workers in America look to international management and marketing opportunities to sustain the high cost of living. The Department of Labor believes nine out of the top 25 jobs over the next ten years will be in technology, and technology opens doors to positions in management and marketing. Recent salary figures show the average computer and information system managers make an average of $126,000 per year. Becoming savvy with technology is fundamental to career success. Only fifteen percent of Fortune 1000 companies are using analytics to improve their relationship with customers and vendors.

Lawrence Peterson

JOBS AS SURROGATE PARENTS

Jobs do more than provide livelihood. Jobs satisfy basic psychological and social needs. In logo parentis is Latin for serving as surrogate parents. From birth through adulthood we are programmed by society to go to school and then on to work. The function of education is to turn out citizens who think, feel and act in predictable patterns. According to R.D. Laing, the best way to manipulate others is to tell them who they are, not what to do. The emphasis on conformity does not encourage self-exploration so job expectations are fairly standardized. Through conditional regard beginning with our family, then school, our thoughts, feelings and actions are prescribed. Regrettably, so are notions of rejection when we deviate from the norm. When the average job seeker follows the norm, opportunities to stand out and reside outside of the norm. If we want greater compensation than the group, we need to find greater obstacles to overcome where creative problem solving is crucial to results. Following the group translates into mundane jobs where creativity is stifled. Answering want ads frequently leads to perfunctory jobs. Successful career candidates create jobs rather than accept position.

Jobs provide earnings and a degree of stimulation through our interaction with coworkers. This is particularly acute in the military. When the job is fulfilling, workers grow in competence and self-esteem. When you like what you do the entire world takes on a positive glow. When work becomes a drudge everyone and everything becomes an annoyance. Since we spend more awake hours on a job than at home with our loved ones, jobs become a source for cognitive stimulation or boredom depending upon the organizational climate. Transformational companies use charisma and expert knowledge to motivate employees. Transactional companies use rewards and punishments and the power of positions to motivate. Collaborative organizations use nurturing to motivate employees. Understand organizational culture is important to finding the right fit. Research clearly indicates a strong relationship between job fit and commitment, satisfaction and turnover.

Regrettably, perfunctory job descriptions are tantamount to slow motion suicide, depriving the brain of stimulation and resulting in lost motivation. Because the ravages of unemployment are emotionally devastating, distasteful jobs are tolerated because they are less stressful than no job at all. Neurasthenic Neurosis describes the depression befalling people who are bored with work. The side-effects are chronic fatigue and a lack of enthusiasm. Why do seniors fight mandatory retirement policies? They fully understand getting dressed and having no place to go leads to a quicker grave than reporting to work each day. Small wonder over two-thirds of senior respondents put their lives and livelihood ahead of spending time with their children.

Research shows incongruities in perceptions between workers and companies when it comes to understanding the demands of a job. Incongruities include prior work experience with similar jobs, the degree to which the worker is willing to cooperate with the requirements of the job, the degree to which the worker understands the requirements of the job and the particular needs and values the worker brings to the job. If you encounter less pay than you need or expect for your contribution, secretly believe you can do better, or find the amount of time you have spent with an organization is not providing an adequate return, it is time to consider a career move.

Experiments in ego depletion have determined each time we

deny ourselves an opportunity for growth we use up valuable reserves leaving us susceptible to learned helplessness. Feelings of helplessness and depression result from the belief we cannot escape aversive circumstances. Questioning our self-efficacy leads to reduced motivation, reduced capacities and reduced mental functioning. Successful job candidates overcome helplessness by understanding conflict leads to growth and strength. General systems theory shows internal control comes from information leading to better choices and additional opportunities for self-sufficiency.

JOB FIT AND PERSONALITY TYPES

Job candidates just entering the work force may have no idea of where they might best fit in. Experienced job candidates would be well served to understand what jobs represent the best fit for occupational fulfillment. The majority of jobs can divided into four main functions; management, sales, accounting and staff. The research of William Marston proposes a DISC model that readily compliments these four functions. If you have encountered organizational resistance in past assignments, it is helpful to compare the assignment with your basic personality style.

Dominance is a personality style related to the need for control, power and assertiveness generally the purview of Management. Descriptions of dominance include being demanding, forceful, strong willed, driving, determined, ambitious, aggressive and pioneering. Dominance is associated with extraversion and Max Lucher's RED personality indicative of strong-willed, strong-minded people who like accepting challenges, taking action, and getting immediate results. If interviewing with a dominant personality type, it is important to understand they respond with greater cooperation when messages are attributed to authority versus anonymous sources.

Inducement is a personality style related to social situations and communication, important qualities for sales. Descriptions of inducement include being convincing, magnetic, political, enthusiastic, persuasive, warm, demonstrative, trusting and optimistic. Inducement is associated with extraversion and Max Lucher's YELLOW personality indicative of people who like participating on teams, sharing ideas, and energizing and entertaining others. When interviewing with an inducement personality type it is important to understand they respond with greater cooperation when messages are geared towards prestige and popularity.

Compliance is a personality style related to caution and conscientiousness both critical to accounting. Descriptions of compliance include careful, cautious, exacting, neat, systematic, diplomatic, accurate and tactful. Consider how well this personality style fits in with accounting and purchasing assignments. Compliance is associated with introversion and Max Lucher's GREEN personality indicative of people who value quality and like planning ahead, employing systematic approaches, and checking and re-checking for accuracy. When interviewing with a compliant personality type it is important to understand they cooperate with the merits of an argument more than the source.

Steadiness is a personality style related to patience, persistence and thoughtfulness as demonstrated by support staff personnel and executive assistants. Descriptions of steadiness include calm, relaxed, patient, possessive, predictable, deliberate, stable and consistent. Steadiness is associated with introversion and Max Lucher's BLUE personality indicative of helpful people who like working behind the scenes, performing in consistent and predictable ways, and who are good listeners.

Each personality lends itself to a job description. Poor fit in unfulfilling jobs frequently results from accepting offers incompatible with basic personality traits. Psychology teaches our basic personality is formed by the age of seven. When we accept assignments incompatible with our basic personality style, we inevitably encounter conflict contributing to work stress. We feel underutilized and unappreciated because our style is does not compliment the needs of the assignment. If you desire additional information regarding your personality style, there are several psychological instruments available. The Myers Briggs, Kiersey Temperament Sorter, 16PF Questionnaire, and Disc Assessment instrument are a few readily found by performing a Google search.

FUTURE SHOCK

Future shock occurs when we are unable to keep up with the incessant demands of change. Even positive change in moving up the organizational ladder is stressful. In paraphrasing the late Armand Hammer, long hours never killed anyone. Heart attacks at an early age stem from the worry associated with corporate politics. Corporate jockeying is beset with unknowns. You can never predict with precision where your political alliances will lead. Occupying icon status with one set of corporate dignitaries suddenly leads to plebe status through restructuring. This inability to predict outcomes leads to anxiety, frustration and anger.

The inability to cope with change and predict outcomes fosters a myriad of mental dysfunctions associated with cognitive dissonance. Workers promoted from the ranks to supervision experience cognitive dissonance when the demands of the new job conflict with the relationships of the prior job. Newly promoted supervisors must either accept the cultural mores of the higher group or experience debilitating stress. Cognitive dissonance is displaced through escape mechanisms like alcohol, drugs, and promiscuity. Frequently, supervisors who cannot adapt are terminated or quit the company because they cannot cope with change. In attempting to function both as a manager and a rank and file worker frequently results in being alienated by both groups.

Group conformity is a powerful weapon used by organizations to ensure compliance with corporate objectives. An experiment was performed by Solomon Asch, whereby participants were asked to determine the length of lines drawn on a paper. What the test participant did not know was the other two participants were confederates whose sole purpose was to convince the test subject the length of the lines were the same, despite the fact they clearly were not. Nearly seventy-five percent of the test subjects changed their perceptions to match the confederates demonstrating the power of conformity and group influence in altering individual perceptions. Listening to economic news can be pessimistic and can easily influence belief systems just like the test subjects in the preceding experiment. News markets negativity and fear. When job candidates buy into negative economic news, they soon develop catastrophic expectations; sending out fewer resumes and going on fewer interviews because they feel they are a waste of time.

Lawrence Peterson

MEASURING YOUR STRESS QUOTIENT

Technology is doubling at an alarming pace and no one remains current for long. It has been suggested if technological research stopped tomorrow; it would still take fifty years to develop what has already being discovered. Since change is inevitable, the only rational recourse is to learn to anticipate change so personal stress becomes manageable. Stress produces a variety of symptoms among individuals. When we feel out of control we experience anxiety, depression and a decline in our physical health. Lab experiments show rats unable to escape shock developed ulcers and people are no different. Learning to identify sources of stress and strategies to avoid it are an important element in achieving career success.

Job stress from a poor job fit or toxic work setting gives rise to Freudian ego defense mechanisms in workers. For example, denial of reality protects the self from unpleasant experience by refusing to see it. Workers who refuse to address the unpleasant elements of their job are only suppressing the stress so it eventually surfaces elsewhere. When we are under stress associated with a toxic job or in between jobs, we frequently seek to discharge our pent up feelings through active or passive aggression towards others. Because we fail to confront the stress, we are not in a position to resolve it. Society conditions us to associate our feelings of worth with companies we work for. When our job is unfulfilling or recognition is absent, we protect our feelings of inadequacy by blaming others for our lack of results. Blaming others is not a productive strategy for resolving stressful issues. Stress can also cause us to regress to earlier levels of emotional development. Our behavior becomes childish or impulsive. A serious side-effect of ego defense mechanisms is fantasy where job seekers engage in magical thinking or the belief in supernatural intervention rather than take active steps to learn how to effectively market their skills in a competitive marketplace. Because ego defense mechanisms are means of denial, they serve to increase stress rather than diminish it. A better approach is to change jobs or find a fulfilling job rewarding contribution so competency and self-esteem grow.

Alexandra Michel, a researcher at University of Southern California recently reported on the stressful effects of investment banking, citing insomnia, alcoholism, heart palpitations, eating disorders, and explosive tempers due to the toxic work atmosphere. This report underscores the growing number of observations citing over a third of all workers in America are unhappy in unmotivated careers.

Because of the natural tendency for denial, stress is not always obvious. There are instruments for measuring stress that help determine the impact on our personal and professional lives. Holmes and Rahe created an instrument entitled the Social Readjustment Rating Scale to measure stress through life style changes. Changes in your daily routine are measured in Life Change Units. A score of 300 suggests a major illness is imminent.

Events and Scale of Impact:

Death of a spouse = 100
Divorce = 73
Marital separation = 65
Jail = 63
Death of a close family member = 63
Personal injury or illness = 53
Marriage = 50
Fired at work = 47
Marital Reconciliation = 45
Retirement = 45
Change in health of family member = 44
Pregnancy = 40
Sex difficulties = 39
Gain of a new family member = 39
Business Readjustment = 39
Change in financial state = 38
Death of close friend = 37
Change to a different line of work = 36
Change in number of arguments with spouse = 35
Mortgage over $10,000 = 31
Foreclosure of mortgage or loan = 30
Change in responsibilities at work = 29
Son or daughter leaving home = 29
Trouble with in-laws = 29
Outstanding personal achievement = 28
Wife begins or stops work = 26
Begin or end school = 26
Change in living conditions = 25
Revision of personal habits = 24
Trouble with boss = 23
Change in work hours or conditions = 20
Change in residence = 20
Change in schools = 20
Change in recreation = 19

Change in church activities = 19
Change in social activities = 18
Mortgage or loan less than $10,000 = 17
Change in sleeping habits = 16
Change in number of family get-togethers = 15
Change in eating habits = 15
Vacation = 13
Christmas = 12
Minor violations of the law = 11.

Add up the points applicable to your situation. If your score is 300 or more, statistics suggest you are headed for a major illness within the next two years.

As you can see from the list scores are assigned to different life events. Items associated with work are relatively obvious. Ancillary connections to work can also be made. Employment problems lead to excessive drinking. If you drive while drinking, "violations of the law" comes into play. Employment problems also affect eating habits, the number of family get-togethers, change in residence, change in living conditions, possible foreclosure on a loan, and the stress of a spouse going to work to pay the incessant volley of bills coming in the mail each month.

Changing jobs or needing to make a change in careers significantly elevates our stress threshold. The decision to remain at work and experience stress, or experience the risk of finding a new job can be daunting. Nevertheless, remaining in a dead end job only serves to prologue the problem. Fighting off depression when looking for another job can also be problematic. When you jotted down the items applicable to you within the last twelve months was your score more than you realized? The impact of unfavorable work conditions, authoritarian supervision, getting passed over for a promotion, family disruptions because of job relocation, competition among co-workers, and excessive driving to get to and from work could easily add to the length of the list. When your life demonstrates a high level of sustained stress, you are vulnerable to a tipping point; a major issue can easily place you in a high threat category for an illness. Small wonder billions are paid annually by workers attempting to treat the symptoms of misery encountered at work or from unemployment. A fulfilling job minimizes negative stress and encourages career growth and better health overall. Learning to identify work opportunities and strategies for change is a fundamental goal of this handbook. Read on.

ONCE YOU'VE LEFT THE MERRY-GO-ROUND

Work annoyances encourage irritability and ulcers. Unemployment can lead to financial ruin, social disgrace, and suicide. A seminal study by Emile Durkheim established a link between suicide rates and social uncertainty. The lack of work can have a devastating financial and psychological impact. The major mechanism behind the growing trend in homelessness is the inability to find a job or meaningful work. People get fed up and drop out. Unemployment follows a vicious circle where self-worth is depreciated because organizational validation is lacking. We are social creatures and when we no longer have the validation of coworkers or a job, we soon begin to question our abilities. The unemployed claim there are not sufficient jobs to go around. Companies complain they cannot find workers. Mismatches and competition are inevitable underscoring the importance of learning how to market your career. Companies compete for their products. Similarly, competition for jobs has become fierce and requires similar marketing tactics if the job seeker is to succeed. The stigma of unemployment is well known. Companies shy away from job candidates who are not working. A recent economic bureau sent out 12,000 fake resumes portraying job candidates as having been out of work anywhere from one month to three years. There was a statistical correlation between the length of time out of work and the call backs. Resumes indicating longer out of work times were less frequently responded to. If you find yourself in between jobs, even a voluntary position looks better on a resume than being out of work and there are numerous positions to be had you can work from home such as customer service or technical support.

Once you've left the work merry-go-round it is difficult to get back on. Women quitting jobs to raise children face obstacles when attempting to return to work. Breaks in work continuity are interpreted by employers as outdated skills. Candidates returning to work frequently take less compensation because the zeitgeist says you must prove your worth all over again. Getting back on the merry-go-round necessitates learning to market and sell your qualifications and ideas as current solutions to problems facing prospective employers. Some problems are universal and timeless. Problems with sales, marketing, inventory control, production management, management information systems, research and development are ongoing in a rapidly growing market. If you can show you have a solution to an organizational problem, the stigma with being in between jobs is no longer an obstacle. Companies will be entranced with your ideas, not your break from continuous employment. Consider seeking part-time work or volunteer work as another possible means of eliminating the unemployment bias.

UNEMPLOYMENT THE ULTIMATE PARIAH

Since work plays such a critical role in physical and mental well-being, finding a better fit within the system is too important to be left to the whims of fate or chance. Remaining in a dead job saps vitality and leads to a decline in our mental health. When our mental health is on the decline we reject potential opportunities for career growth. This symptom has been called learned helplessness. The concept of learned helplessness was coined by Martin Seligman based upon his work with dogs. Through a process called classical conditioning, dogs were given an electric shock after hearing a tone. Soon thereafter, the dogs made no attempt to escape the shock, having learned to behave in a helpless manner. When workers feel they have limited control over situations, they begin to behave in a helpless manner, overlooking opportunities for change. Learned helplessness is associated with anxiety, depression, loneliness, shyness and phobias. When workers experience learned helplessness, they believe their actions will not allow them to achieve a better job. They tend to stick with high stress jobs that do not reward their contribution to the point of termination. Once terminated, learned helplessness rears its ugly head once again and prevents job candidates from believing they deserve a better job.

Many workers believe finding positions with major companies automatically guarantees continued employment. Regrettably, hostile takeovers, mergers and acquisitions cause tremendous upheaval for millions of workers forcing them to reassess their career options. The first thing a raiding company revamps is management. The first rule of business for new management is to reorganize the staff. Cronyism is rampant because new management prefers to bring aboard people they have history with and believe they can rely on. In this sense, a known is preferred over an unknown. Golden Parachutes and outplacement counseling are euphemisms for "Pack your bags, you're fired!" Although working for a start-up company promises growth opportunities, consider only one in twelve companies make it past the first year. Survival in the market place demands job seekers become adept agents of change. Customers make decisions based upon emotional and rational appeals to their personality. Company decision makers can likewise be induced to make purchasing decisions in the form of job offers. Once you understand what the magician knows, you have control over the magic. In career terms, learning behavioral strategies for elevated interpersonal competence significantly boosts your opportunities in the market place. Savvy career candidates no longer harbor the fear associated with find a new job because they have mastered the fundamentals of interpersonal persuasion. So can you.

THE RISE OF THE GLOBAL CORPORATION

Reducing labor costs is the sole basis behind companies who move their manufacturing and assembly plants offshore where labor rates are low. To increase profits, layoffs and high unemployment are inevitable. World consumers refuse to pay for products inflated by the labor rates of rich countries. The rise of the Multi-national Corporation means loyalty to a given workforce is no longer a corporate concern. The sole goal of the Board of Directors is to satisfy investors. Increasing profitability inevitably leads to layoffs. Pass through taxation means products manufactured in other countries can be passed through to the United States and not pay taxes because the profits were extracted from the product in the country where the product was manufactured. Because the assets of large multinational corporations exceeds the budgets of small countries, there is a strong incentive for multinational companies to employ workers in smaller countries with low tax rates and then inflate the selling price before it is exported to countries like the United States. This strategy contributes to unemployment in countries with high standards of living.

Because of the high standard of living in the United States,

Peter Drucker suggested the future of American workers resides in international management and marketing positions. Emerging third world countries need specialized expertise in brand management, marketing, sales, customer service and technical support, workers without borders is rapidly becoming a viable alternative. Companies like Apple, AOL, Atari, Bacardi, Boeing, Chevron, Coca Cola, Dell, Facebook, General Electric, Halliburton, IBM, Johnson and Johnson, McDonalds, Michelin, Microsoft, Nestle, Pepsico, Sony, Starbucks and Wal-Mart are multinational. When considering working for a multinational corporation, consider how valuable any additional language skills will become in marketing your background and qualifications.

THE INFORMATION AGE

What began with Samuel Morse's original telegraph transmitter has become a multi-billion dollar business enterprise known as the computer age. Computers have profoundly changed the way we do business with the ability to transfer information instantly around the globe. Similar to the shift from a trad-itional industry to the industrial revolution, the information society welcomes the advent of numerous microminiaturiza-tion advances for the information age. The Internet provides a network for connecting computers for information gathering, email and file transfers giving rise to the phenomena known as the World Wide Web. Consumers now have access to vast librar-ies of information at the mere click of a mouse. The impact on jobs has altered the work landscape with employments shifting away from manufacturing and towards tasks related to service. Cybercrime is creating enormous opportunities for hackers and security firms to prevent data theft. Farmers are using data to keep track of weather to anticipate the best time to grow crops.

Physicians can access databases with patient medical records to provide timely diagnosis and treatment both locally and in concert with other physicians in other countries. Computers have allowed us to sequence the human genome and provide medicines to a wide range of diseases. Consider over 24 hours of video are uploaded to YouTube every minute of every day. With the advent of social media tools, workers can cultivate promising business contacts. There is no doubt video games will be fashioned along work requirements so work becomes play. This is already happening in some antivirus programs.

Not only is information big business, the equipment in support of the information age generates billions of dollars annually from the sale of personal computers, cellular phones and tablets being used as computers and quasi fax machines. There is power in information and America has become the leading purveyor of information on the planet and information consumes a lion share of energy. Huge data rooms are filled with computers drawing the equivalent of 30 nuclear power plants worldwide to sustain our preoccupation with immediate information. Data rooms have battery and generator backups to ensure the steady flow of information and the demand is growing. Apple computer has recently taken over the number one position in profitability and sales. The various ways Information is packaged becomes an indispensable catalyst in moving products and services across the planet. Information and smart phone applications are now being fine tuned to the end user. Marketing companies are using computer GPS to track consumers along with their purchases. Credit card companies routinely sell the information they glean from credit card sales. Super markets share your purchasing information so marketing companies can flood you with offers to buy products or decide what product gets additional facing on the shelf.

Emulating the strategies successful companies have used to sell their products and services allows job candidates to become more successful at career marketing. Riding the information wave is crucial for survival in a modern economy. Consider posting your resume on Monster.com, 4jobs, CareerBuilder, Hotjobs, HotResumes, Job.com, Resumerabbit, Jobstand, The Ladders, JobCity, Jobing, Thingamajob, Dice, and many more with a click of the mouse. PC Magazine recently posted the top search sites as Indeed, SimplyHired, LinkedIn, CareerBuilder, Monster, Craigslist, Glassdoor, Dice, Mediabistro, and TweetMy-Jobs. Finding a job or changing careers has been simplified with the information age. Job candidates can let their computers perform much of the leg work, allowing more time to research and follow up on quality opportunities.

NEW WORKER EXPECTATIONS

The days of scientific management principles where people are treated like machines is over. Workers have not become the machines of mass information through the use of computers and smart phones. Technologically savvy workers no longer come to work merely for a paycheck. They now expect work to provide a greater meaning and opportunities for the expression of creativity. Unlike mathematics, languages or the humanities, we are rarely taught about creativity, despite its importance to our lives. Consider the worker who came up with the idea of selling donut holes. The information and opportunities are out there, waiting to be used. Workers now demand autonomy, participation, involvement, recognition, stability and expression. More than any times in history workers are expecting a job to help them improve their skills, provide opportunities for promotion, provide progress towards their career goals and provide the leadership for job stability. Dead end perfunctory jobs is the primary reason workers jump to new positions with alarming frequency. Turnover statistics with some organizations is embarrassing and reflects incompetent management refusing to value diversity, who are intolerant to differences, and who are closed to new ideas.

An interesting experiment was performed whereby a maintenance worker was asked to dig a series of holes in a field adjacent to the factory where he worked without additional explanation from the supervisor. After digging several holes and then instructed to fill the holes the maintenance frustrated worker finally quit. At the root of the problem was the absence of communication. Had the supervisor informed the worker they were looking for an underground valve, the circumstances would have been dramatically different. Workers want information so they can feel competent in performing their tasks. Authoritarian management practices frequently alienate the worker resulting in high employee turnover.

The first question a job candidate should ask a company why is the position open and what happened to the incumbent. Not only do toxic work atmospheres encourage job hopping, high turnover is further induced by rapidly changing markets. Companies rise and fall with alarming regularity and positions soon become obsolete because of changing technology. Colleges and Universities tailor academic programs to satisfy the needs of the market place but can no longer keep abreast of change. Frequently, the skills students learn in school are obsolete when they finally graduate. Community colleges are now tailoring specialized programs for the market place, because two years reduces obsolescence over four year programs.

Job retraining has become a necessity and learning new job marketing skills is an absolute requisite to remain vital and competitive in the workplace. Rapid market shifts leave unprepared workers confused, insecure and in a high risk health profile due to the impact of stress. According to an American Community Survey in 2010, over 45 million people lived in a different house the prior year. We have become a transient society due to the ebb and flow of the global economy. The high incidence of divorce reflects the ravages of unemployment and added tension brought about by adjusting to a new job or poor working conditions. On the one hand experts suggest a sellers' market is emerging because baby boomers are leaving the workforce. On the other hand, workers are delaying retirement or taking low paying entry level jobs after retirement, once the bailiwick of high school and college students. A major transition in the workforce is also being witnessed. Blue collar positions are being replaced by white collar jobs as robotics becomes more commonplace in manufacturing. Company tenure is giving way to situational problem solvers who can readily improve operational and organizational efficiency caused by rapid change. Change is ubiquitous and incessant. This is favorable news for candidates who learn the anticipate change and adopt effective fundamentals of lifelong career marketing.

COLLEGE DEGREES

Although college has been touted as the fast track for increasing lifelong compensation, there are disadvantages in attending college. Time spent earning a degree represents a loss of immediate earnings. If you specialize in your degree program you might find the information obsolete by the time you graduate. Since most must take out a loan for college, debt is unavoidable. Currently over one-fourth of college graduates are employed in jobs that do not require a college degree. The majority of college freshmen who graduated in the lower half of their high school class will not even make it to college graduation. Because of the high cost associated with education and the ever increasing drop-out rate, alternatives to college are emerging. Trade schools, apprentice programs, and community service and becoming a self-employed entrepreneur. Interestingly, computer technicians can easily earn more money than many educated professionals. Vocational programs for nursing, home health, customer service and retail do not require college degrees. Being self-employed does not generally require a college credentials.

For those who can afford to attend college, graduates soon realize colleges fail to teach how to get a job once they complete their degree program. Graduating from a big name school does not necessarily promise suitable work. Even the allure of the MBA Degree is being offset by companies reluctant to hire new graduates due to economic uncertainty. Graduates are finding themselves in a Catch-22, unable to land a good job because of lack of experience, and unable to get experience because they cannot get hired.

High school students are finding it difficult to secure work because companies have found it beneficial to hire senior citizens who will work for minimum wage. Senior Citizens are perceived as more dependable because they still subscribe to the traditional work ethic. Casual jobs like mowing lawns have been institutionalized by landscape companies and even collecting aluminum cans has become big business. Graduating students who cannot find a job take out more loans to seek advanced degrees, gambling the market will be more receptive with a graduate degree. It is ironic colleges and universities do not place more emphasis on job marketing to leverage degrees into a sustainable livelihood.

The military is still a viable option for those who want training and upward mobility in rank. Many programs allow or encourage college attendance. Skills learned in the military can convert to skills in the civilian marketplace. Frequently, skills acquired in the military can be leveraged into civilian jobs in defense, security and intelligence gathering. An interesting development involves radio control. The four branches of the military are now encouraging anyone with radio control experience to enlist and undergo additional training for use in drone programs. Drones are also becoming popular in civilian markets for diverse uses. Farmers use drones to check on crops. Ranchers use drones to check on their herds. The forestry service uses drones to check on fires. Electric companies use drones to check on utility pole status. Law enforcement uses drones for surveillance. Real estate professionals are using drones to take overhead photos of properties to enhance sales saving thousands of dollars over hiring a pilot to obtain arial photographs. Drones are becoming smaller and their use is becoming more widespread. Undoubtedly, drones will soon be delivering medication to shut-ins. Learning radio control was once a hobby; now a growing career option.

Since a degree is known to open doors to career opportunities and earning power there are alternate ways to earn a degree discussed in a subsequent chapter under "Substitutes for Education."

INTERPERSONAL SKILLS FOR CAREER ADVANCEMENT

Interpersonal psychology has become the prerequisite for adapting to the labor needs of the modern economy. Interpersonal relations are the magic shibboleth for work advancement and employees promoted to the higher positions are frequently not the most technically competent but certainly the most persuasive. Frequently interpersonal resistance stems from a fear of loss of control or feelings of vulnerability. Getting offers requires compliance from the decision maker. Compliance gaining strategies include the promise of benefits, being helpful, and appealing to positive self-esteem. Punishment strategies suggest a loss of value or reward can also be useful for the accomplished communicator; by suggesting a company hire you because you can keep them from losing money.

The principles of consumer and marketing psychology can add to personal control by anticipating, identifying and exploiting specific niches in the market. If consumer psychology works for selling goods and services, it certainly works for job candidates representative of products and services. Modern statistics show it takes the average worker two years to find another position. New positions generally pay less than the prior positions. Understanding how to identify the right company and offer strategic incentives can significantly reduce time between jobs and ensure elevated compensation. Over ninety percent of job seekers follow traditional means for securing work and end up in dead-end jobs with little to no opportunity for advancement. They flock to the want ads or employment agencies and volunteer to be underutilized. It doesn't have to be that way!

Consider the advantages of being self-employed, becoming a consultant, working several part-time jobs and paid internships as alternatives to want ad job seeking. Volunteer jobs are an excellent platform for networking with decision makers who might hire you or serve as a source for being hired by another organization. Part-time positions are defined as those offering up to thirty hours per week and between 3 to eight hours at a time. Part-time positions frequently pay well and are win-win, providing employment and helping companies who need the bases covered in the evenings or on weekends. Consider investigating online opportunities at Groovejob, Hotrecruit, Indeed, Mom Corps, Laborready, Monster, and SnagAJob for starters. Part-time positions are readily available in health care, retail, customer relations, sales, advertising, bookkeeping, data entry, production, hospitality, security, loss prevention, trucking, teaching, and warehousing.

TYPEWRITERS ARE US

Although ten percent of all candidates increase their career competence through formal assistance and training, most career instruction recommends strategies adopted in the past. Traditional approaches to finding work are like recommending typewriters when keyboards have become the accepted norm. Typewriters were a giant step beyond the quill pen. Typewriters are antiques compared to modern computers and cell phones with virtual keyboards. It seems ages ago when Isaac Asimov encouraged writers to throw away their typewriters and adopt computers because of the time saving advantages. Little did he know keyboards would become commonplace in the majority of households. Examples of obsolescence include looking up phone numbers in a book, waiting to get photos developed, Polaroids, tractor fed printing paper, paper with carbons, buying a new car with a cigarette lighter, wearing a calculator watch, watching a VCR, dialing on a rotary phone, using a public phone booth, storing information on a floppy disk, booting from a C:/ prompt or chatting with a SysOp. Not long ago we laughed at eight tracks in favor of cassette tapes. Then cassettes gave way to CD's. Now CD's are obsolete. Similarly, gone are PDA's, movie rental stores, maps, land lines, and long-distance charges.

Every generation is faced with obsolescence. We no longer ride a horse to get around town or turn a crank to start a car. We no longer light a fire to start a stove or hang clothes on a line to dry. We now carry information on a memory stick, transfer information by pointing our phone, access the World Wide Web through Wi-Fi hotspots, speak to type, and chat with customers and friends through our car stereo. How the world has changed in such a short amount of time.

Just as old equipment and processes are no longer adaptable to the current needs of the market, traditional employment strategies are no longer relevant for upwardly mobile job candidates. Approaching companies solely from advertisements is like using a typewriter without a zip drive; lots of work and minimal benefit. By implementing the job search principles advocated in this handbook job candidates are relegated to the upper two percentile of the population ahead of the competition still following traditional job search strategies. Adapt your career skills to emerging markets and leave obsolescence to the lemmings following one another off of the cliff of mediocrity. Enjoy the freedom and happiness in finding a job that fits your personality and interests. Approach interviews with confidence because you have learned the mechanics of interpersonal persuasion.

Lawrence Peterson

NOTHING MOVES UNTIL SOMETHING IS SOLD

Fortunes are made because someone has something to sell. Lawyers sell knowledge, parking garages sell space, physicians sell health, designers sell concepts and insurance companies sell security. Much like successful product and service corporations, the key to finding the job you want involves sales and marketing. Cyrus McCormick grew up on a Virginia farm in the eighteen hundreds and went on to invent innovative farm equipment. When farmers balked at the higher prices associated with the new farm equipment, Cyrus used consumer psychology by offering installment buying when the competition still insisted on cash. Cyrus understood the importance of customer contact and went on to be the first to place sales representatives in the field to demonstrate his company's farm equipment. Richard Warren Sears showed an understanding of psychology when he donated catalogues to schools as reading primers. An entire generation of students was taught to read from the Sears Catalogue and went on to become loyal consumers. Successful marketers offer incentives. Modern job candidates follow similar strategies when they offer creative incentives and solutions to companies. The very fabric of the economy is based on supply and demand. When competition reduces demand, savvy marketing professionals come up with new ideas to place their products foremost in the mind of the consumer. Successful marketers have learned to distinguish their products and services from the competition with promises to solve problems and so can you.

Consider how tennis shoes were once simple canvas shoes with rubber soles. Modern tennis shoes are called athletic shoes and are differentiated into numerous sport specialties, from tennis to skate boarding, and come with diverse features and benefits for the consumer. Product differentiation is achieved through physical differences, perceived differences and differences in service. The famous taste test between Coca Cola and Pepsi attempts to show consumers choose Pepsi when deprived of the physical appearance of the Coca Cola can and familiar logo. The perception among Coca Cola drinkers is their brand is superior to other brands. A simple blind fold test removed the brand bias. Similarly, job candidates can run into brand bias when companies prefer graduates from specific backgrounds and universities. Savvy job candidates point to their exceptional differences to encourage value and reduce prejudicial bias. Selling unique expertise changes interview dynamics. Notice how Apple created a competitive advantage by offering the MacBook Air as the lightest and thinnest laptop on the market despite hundreds of other brands being offered. Job candidates can borrow the strategy used by Apple by marketing their unique problem solving skills as rapid solutions. During prohibition bootleggers outsmarted their competition by calling moonshine, "White Lightening," conveying how their liqueur was superior to other suppliers. Consider how including, "Solve your production problems in thirty days or less," allows employers to differentiate you from other job candidates.

SELL THE SIZZLE

Alfred P. Sloan coined the phrase, "Sell the sizzle, not the steak," to emphasize people do not purchase products, the buy benefits. Just as programs must be geared to the needs of potential consumers, job candidates must gear their backgrounds to the needs of employers. Consider the catch phrase used by the Holiday Inn, "Pleasing people the world over," to emphasize their emphasis on customer satisfaction. A toothpaste company reached millions of consumers with their slogan, "You'll wonder where the yellow went when you brush your teeth with Pepsodent." Kellogg's Rice Krispy was famous for their unforgettable slogan, "Snap! Crackle! Pop! Each of the preceding examples evokes a hook connected with a benefit in the mind of the consumer. Similarly, getting job offers involves strategically adapting your skills and abilities as hooks to respective firms. People do not purchase rain coats, the buy the benefit of staying dry. Necessity has been called the mother of invention. McDonalds began by converting a barbecue restaurant into a successful hamburger chain by applying modern production assembly line principles to food preparation. Interestingly, the procedures were identical to what the White Castle hamburger chain had been using for the previous twenty years. The sizzle in this context was "fast food," and the promise has ushered in a new era of convenience. Regarding convenience, consider the growing number of convenience stores popping up across America. Their prices are not highly competitive because they are not selling price. They are selling the benefit of being easily accessible. Years ago a grocery store decided to remain open 24 hours a day. Interestingly, sales during the evening did not pick up dramatically. Amazingly, sales during the day increased dramatically. Why? Because customers responded to the convenience of being able to purchase products night or day! The next leap in service will undoubtedly involve home delivery of products creating new employment opportunities throughout America.

Medical centers were innovations adopted by physicians, pharmacies and laboratories to offer convenience to their patients. They realized they had a captive audience and most patients would take advantage of products and services offered on the premises rather than drive to another location. Similarly, dentists adopt offices adjacent to orthodontists and feed one another patients. Convenience is a strong incentive, particularly in considering part-time work opportunities. Being able to work weekends and evenings is an asset to many companies. Likewise, being able to work from home is an asset to employees. Because of reciprocal benefits, part-time employment is a growing trend in the marketplace.

The creation of the calculator, computer, cell phone, digital pad and related inventions were adapted to the workplace and marketed to reduce toil and improving performance. Where draftsmen once used paper and pencil to create their drawings, technology subsequently introduced tape to be applied to plastic backgrounds. The sizzle illustrated how tape could be changed quickly for rapid blueprints without having to redraw the entire work. Tape became obsolete with the advent of pointing devices and digital drawing boards. The new sizzle involved the ability to rapidly draw an object using CADCAM three dimensional data easily converted into a computer program for use with multi-station automated machining. The next step in the evolution of machining will involve 3D printers able to create products from digital files. With such printers you can buy, sell and create custom products opening up a completely new market for the home enterprise.

Each step in the innovative process opened doors to new employment opportunities using features and benefits as the hook to move products and services. Each time a new product is created the wheels of progress move and open doors to new jobs. Getting job offers requires understanding and anticipating innovation and subsequently selling the sizzle in the form of future benefits. By packaging your qualifications as benefits adapted to the immediate and future needs of the company, a higher frequency of offers will result. Consider language companies exploiting the growth in global trade by offering to teach a language in as little as thirty days. The sizzle is being able to open doors to new opportunities through your newly acquired language skills. Read on. Your approach to finding work will soon be changed forever.

MARKETING PSYCHOLOGY

Psychology paints rosy pictures of castles in the sky. Marketing shows how to rent them.

THE FOUR P'S OF MARKETING

Marketing traditionally rests atop four pillars: Product, Price, Placement and Promotion. Once the product has been conceived the question is how the product can be produced at an affordable price. For example, despite knowing how to desalinate water, we still accept drought conditions throughout the country because the process is considered too expensive. Recently the town of Marina, California shuttered their seven million dollar desalination plant because they felt converting clean drinking water from salt water would not provide a favorable return on investment. As drought conditions worsen and technology improves, the need for drinking water will offset the perception of price and desalination programs will offer employment opportunities for the observant job seeker. We are willing to pay more for what we value. The price of Ben and Jerry's ice cream sells for more than generic ice cream because consumers are willing to pay more for what the perceived higher quality ice cream. Similarly, job candidates representing greater perceived value to an organization receive higher compensation.

Once product and price have been established the third decision involves identifying markets where the product will be sold. If consumption is minimal the price will be higher to cover the investment of making the product. Similarly, if a job candidate's skill is valuable and scarce, compensation will be higher. If the demand is widespread the product can be standardized to reduce the price and increase profitability. Likewise, if the demand for a particular job is low like many entry level positions, compensation is generally low.

Demand can be manipulated through the strategic use of psychology. Once the product, price and market have been identified a promotion is created to apprise the consumer of benefits strategically portrayed to elicit a favorable response. Generally consumers buy for emotional purposes so companies use focused strategies designed to increase consumer demand and response. "Ring Around the Collar," was a successful marketing campaign in the seventies used by Lever Brothers to create consumer anxiety evoked by the thought of an unsightly ring around the shirt collar. To minimize the anxiety, the promise of removing the stain facilitated the sale of Wisk cleaning products. Similarly, the fear of being charged exorbitant prices by a plumber allowed Liquid Plumber to market a DIY drain cleaner. Fear elicits demand for a solution. When job candidates strategically offer their qualifications as services for overcoming organizational problems, their employment demand goes up as well as their compensation.

Have you noticed how car sales representatives encourage potential buyers to take a test drive? They are not being generous. They realize a test drive increases emotional appetite over intellectual objections like price and affordability? In retail a study determined more sales were made when a product was physically placed in the hand of a consumer than when the product was merely pointed to on a shelf. In Freudian terms, the Id demands immediate gratification to have a benefit now, thereby cancelling out the Superego calling for a rational decision. Wise marketing professionals and seasoned sales closers appeal to the emotions of the Id to keep consumers from procrastinating. Because sales and marketing programs are designed to illicit immediate gratification, credit has become the tool allowing consumers to get what they want without having to wait until they can afford to pay cash. What has this to do with career marketing? Job candidates who promise immediate contributions fare better at getting offers than candidates who suggest they need time to develop solutions.

Sometimes information derived from research can increase opportunities in another market. Water is a good example. It has been estimated over 500,000 gallons of water is invested in every pound of beef we consume due to the enormous water demands of oats, grain, and grass grown for livestock. This finding has created opportunities for new methods in agriculture and animal husbandry. On the one hand the price of beef is going up because of the scarcity of water. On the other hand, new market opportunities are surfacing recommending water conservation to grow crops directly for humans so the exhaustible water table of the central plains can be preserved. Consider the implications for agricultural products, research, development, manufacturing, marketing, product demonstrations, and financing derived from the need to innovate water conservation.

Convenience, athletics and growing water awareness have given rise to the current explosion in bottled water sales. We discussed how we are willing to pay more for what we value. Consider the millions of dollars spent on bottled water and plastics disposal. The popularity of bottled drinking water has encouraged growth in companies converting plastic bottles into recyclable plastic. To capitalize on perceived needs associated with a green planet and ecology, water filter companies are touting their products as being less expensive overall and providing cleaner water than what you get from a bottle without the collateral waste. All industries, including governments, use marketing persuasion to educate consumers and move products and services. Likewise, savvy career professionals study horizontal and vertical product and service integrations to present upcoming job opportunities. Vertical integration involves following a product from its origin to the end user. In the preceding example, tracing water from the source to the end user follows a number of steps. Job candidates can decide at what level they want to apply their talents. Water reclamation, water processing, plastic bottle manufacturing, warehousing, marketing, sales, vending machines, merchandising, and water route sales are but a few examples.

SALES VERSUS MARKETING

Marketing involves reaching and persuading consumers and typically includes direct mail broadcasts and advertising. Resumes involve marketing; sales involve interpersonal interaction for purposes of employment. In marketing the emphasis is to pull consumers; or encourage decision makers to grant interviews. In sales the emphasis is on pushing or persuading consumers to purchase products and services; or encouraging decision makers to make job offers. Companies use both sales and marketing to move goods and so do job candidates. Where marketing identifies consumer needs and focuses on advertising to generate leads, job candidates send out resumes to generate interviews. Companies perform needs assessments to identify products demonstrating high consumer demand. Likewise, job candidates identify companies demonstrating demand for their services.

Understanding the difference between actual and perceived needs helps job candidates generate more interview enthusiasm. The stronger a perceived need the greater the likelihood a buy or hire decision will be made. Crime is rising but not everyone perceives the need to purchase a burglar alarm system. Faced with creating need for their products, alarm companies conduct presentations in high crime areas to enhance the perceived need of their security systems. The emphasis is on loss prevention. Similarly, the effectiveness of job interviews can be enhanced when job candidates market their background and experience in areas where a perceived need can be exploited. Loss prevention in an employment context includes security, warehousing, accounting, finance, engineering and management; all geared in one way or another to preventing losses to the company. Engineers are frequently hired to build obsolescence into products, cutting costs on materials while ensuring a product continues to work during its warranty period. Consider spray bottles and how the siphon function once worked for years so consumers could reuse bottles for other products. These days a siphon spray bottle barely works long enough to empty the bottle. Manufacturers did not want their spray bottles used for other products so they hired engineers to find a way to create obsolescence in the bottle so they are quickly discarded once the produce is expended.

As an adjunct to obsolescence, pharmaceutical companies pay employees to create pharmaceuticals providing relief but not cure. Patients continually purchase maintenance medication to alleviate their symptoms. Each prescription represents obsolescence. If cures were found pharmaceutical companies would soon go out of business. Adopting a cynical profit strategy encourages pharmaceutical companies to spend millions of dollars on research to moderate symptoms but not eradicate them. Job candidates who seek work with pharmaceutical companies must realize the limitations of their job description. Any innovations promising cures are locked away because they threaten the very livelihood of the organization.

Car dealerships make more profit in their service departments than their sales departments. Each department has its unique objectives that must compliment the overall mission of the company. Car dealers provide work opportunities for sales, custodial staff, accounting staff, finance staff, service writers, part department staff in addition to the technical staff who actually perform work on the cars. Trainers are needed to ensure mechanics are current with new model technology. Regional service managers ensure cost control regarding factory warranties. Corporate headquarters provide support to the dealers in addition to writing policies and procedures while providing marketing and dealer management training. Marketing, advertising and trade show presentations requires hiring professional models to enhance consumer appeal. Car manufacturers provide research, development and specialized troubleshooting for new products and warranty issues. Research and development includes chemists to test plastics, engineers for suspension and much more. Cars undergo safety collision tests which include engineers and scientists trained in physics. There are always department managers who direct, integrate and interpret the findings of the various departments. Each level provides career opportunities for employment.

Managers tend to generalize their qualifications to appeal to the staff directing needs of various companies. Game developers would take a narrower approach to finding work within companies involved preproduction designing, programming, animation, sound design, production, prototype testing and public relations. Opportunities with game companies exist for a diverse number of job candidates, including artists, 3D illustrators, design engineers and digital music producers. Less obvious opportunities include DIY books on gaming strategies, online universities teaching game programming and design, product placement specialists, and trade show staff support to teach consumers about the features and benefits of a particular game. Virtual golf offers products for both online and on site golf systems ranging from a few hundred dollars to several thousands of dollars. Consider taking advantage of your love for golf and applying it to the sale, service and support of such growing enterprises for personal and professional gain. Savvy job candidates become adept at capitalizing on opportunities generally overlooked by the average individual. The difference between a mundane job and a rewarding career involves the ability to see connections in the marketplace. Each market strata has its unique needs. By applying your background and creative energies to the needs of employers, your contributions will be rewarded.

Lawrence Peterson

CUSTOMERS AND EMPLOYERS BUY HOPEFUL EXPECTATIONS

Although customers buy hopeful expectations, even unrealistic expectations are frequently marketed. Car companies have successfully sold muscle cars to thrill seeking consumers by emphasizing speeds far beyond legal speed limits. Consumers buy burglar alarms with the promise of keeping their possessions safe. A glue company suspends a man from his work helmet to emphasize the strength of the bond. A savvy drill bit manufacturer pointed out customers do not buy drill bits, they purchase holes. Job candidates can easily apply the 4 P's of marketing to their careers. You essentially are the product. The placement is the company you seek to work for. The price is the compensation you desire. The Promotion involves your marketing campaign leading to an interview. Marketing campaigns vary. At one end of the bell curve are candidates relying solely on resumes in response to advertised openings. On the other end of the bell curve are candidates performing needs assessments through informational interviews. Like professional marketing organizations the success of your campaign depends upon your ability to accurately identify employer perceived needs and address those needs during your marketing campaign and interview.

Products can represent a complex cluster of value satisfactions. Customers consciously and unconsciously attach value to products in relation to the perceived benefit products represent. Research shows consumers eat more when food is labeled low fat. The perceived benefits are better health and weight loss. Because weight loss is a hot button for consumers, companies have begun to label their products lite when the only thing lite about the product is the color. Because of deceptive packaging practices, laws are being adopted to prevent labeling a product light when the fat content proves otherwise.

An interesting example of perceived benefits involves tape worm diets for consumers desperate to lose weight. Customers are given a treatment of beef tapeworms which interfere with digestion and absorption of nutrients. Unfortunately, the parasite also competes for vitamins and other important nutrients and can cause cysts on the liver, eyes, brain and spinal cord. Nevertheless, the perceived benefits are so attractive to some consumers; they readily opt for the procedure. Because of the health liability, the procedure is illegal in the United States.

Weight loss and thinking small has been exploited in marketing with great success. Miller Lite suggests their product tastes great but is less filling. You might recall the advertising of Clairol hair products that asked the question, "Dies She or Doesn't She?" to suggest their hair products are so natural no one will notice you color your hair. Volkswagen was highly successful by encouraging consumers to "Think small," and Nike has sold millions of shoes by emphasizing, "Just Do it." American Express developed a highly successful slogan with, Don't Leave Home Without it." A very successful marketing campaign to increase milk consumption merely asked, "Got Milk?"

When job candidates accept the fact they are the product, they begin to consider how to market themselves for maximum business appeal. Creative job candidates can customize their cover letters to add marketing hooks much like manufacturers. Try adding "Got Profit?" to the top of your cover letter and see the response you get. The point is to begin approaching companies with similar incentives used successfully by companies to promote their products.

It is important to point out the difference between a well written resume and cover letter and one that involves a fraudulent promise of perceived benefits. Learning to spot opportunities and problems in the marketplace allows for customized approaches that will influence decision makers to grant interviews. If sufficient incentive is present during the interview, a job offer generally follows. Promising benefits that cannot be delivered is self-defeating and will not result in personal or professional growth.

When resumes and cover letters promise value through strategically written qualifications, companies respond in the same way consumers respond when they purchase products. Sending your resume to companies in a broadcast approach is inefficient marketing. Focusing on specific companies and documenting likely needs allows your qualifications to be converted into enticing solutions. Substantial solutions offer greater compensation. Marketing campaigns without solutions take what they can get.

REAL VERSUS IMAGINED PROBLEMS

A food company once marketed the perfect cake mix needing only water. Sales were surprisingly stunted and marketing executives scrambled to find out why. No cooking pride was derived when merely mixing water with batter to get a cake. The manufacturer returned to a recipe requiring other ingredients, like milk and eggs, and sales jumped. The company solved the wrong problem.

An albacore tuna company once launched a successful marketing campaign suggesting their tuna did not turn red in the can. Inferring albacore did not turn into Bonita was a good idea but was quickly labeled brand disparagement and the campaign was stopped. Bonita tuna is naturally red. Suggesting albacore tuna is superior is legal. Suggesting red tuna is spoiled was not. In this example the company attempted to capitalize on an imagined problem that did not exist.

Learn to solve the right problem. Discussing how employers can increase sales when the firm is faced with more orders than it can ship prevents orders. Better strategies propose ways to improve distribution. An instrument company once needed an industrial engineer to facilitate productivity. The engineer cursorily looked over the assembly department and saw the problem. Employees were over handling the product and wasting time. He pointed out the remedy by suggesting a new assembly layout. An offer quickly resulted.

A candidate applied for an engineering position with a manufacturing company experiencing problems with paint adhesion on their products. During a plant walk through, he jotted down the name of the paint they used and called the manufacturer. One of the paint manufacturer's engineers returned his call and gave him the solution to the problem in less than an hour. The solution was a phone call away. Why didn't the company call the manufacturer? The boss was undoubtedly too busy.

Lawrence Peterson

IDENTIFICATION AND JOB OFFERS

Successful marketing programs accurately identify consumer needs. The success of your job search requires you accurately identify perceived company needs. Identification means to associate an internal picture with an object in the external world. Employers quickly learn to identify with their companies, relating to the firm as an extension of themselves. Similarly, workers perceive their jobs as extensions of their personality. Engineers seek jobs with structure and logic. Artists find structure excessively rigid and prefer jobs requiring creativity and intuition. Engineers will be relatively precise, whereas artists will be colorfully and unconventionally creative. Engineers and artists would not find fulfillment if they attempted to swap jobs. The corporate setting they seek will necessitate they package their qualifications to complement their personalities.

Consider the first question typically asked in a social gathering is, "What do you do." Job titles communicate extensive information about your social hierarchy, education, salary, prestige and personality. Marketing companies focus on consumer occupations because they provide rich insights into lifestyle and purchasing patterns. Grocery markets continually compile information regarding purchasing preferences in given demographic areas so as to customize product mix. Customers in one geographical area might be price conscious. Customers in another geographical area would be more concerned with product selection. By compiling purchasing information, grocery markets establish inventories and adjust pricing to their audience. Consumer information is subsequently sold to product manufacturers so they can fine tune their marketing and advertising campaigns. Consider the focus of product coupons and how coupon products are determined.

Where grocery stores are compiling information about purchases, job candidates compile information about job openings and adapt their skills and abilities to compliment the needs and requirements of the organization. Volvo built a solid sales record exploiting the consumer's desire for safety. Volvo geared ads to parents who would appreciate the engineered collision characteristics of the car. Features like childproof rear doors was an important marketing benefit. An interesting example of perceived benefit involves the screen covers for cellular iPhones. The screen on an iPhone is virtually scratchproof and does not require a protective cover. Nevertheless, sly manufacturers have found they can exploit the fear of scratching the display to sell their protective plastic screen covers. Consider the number of consumers ironing out air bubbles to get the plastic screen covers to fit on their cell phone displays. Also consider the amount of profit made by exploiting consumer fear. Perceived benefits are more powerful than actual benefits. Vanity sizing in clothing is a good example. By inserting a label on clothes suggesting a dress is a size four rather than a size eight, more sales are made by complimenting the vanity of the customer. In this case the actual benefit is intangible. The perceived benefit has resulted in millions of sales.

Understanding the style of a company can be helpful in the approach job candidates take with their resume and their interview. Generally, an interview for an engineering position will be quite formal with emphasis on technical details and command of the science. An interview for an artist or illustrator position will tend to be less formal with emphasis on creativity and a portfolio. It is not what you do for a living, but how society feels about what you do for a living that is significant. Old style resume formats and applications place emphasis on job titles and overlook potentialities. Your former job title is used by companies, like a Divine Chain of Being, to fit you into positions they may have available. Similarly, the compensation is pretty much established.

If your last position was rank and file and you now desire a shot at management, your former title works against your ambitions. Since former job descriptions list general tasks and responsibilities, they can type cast a job candidate who desires more responsibility. Listing job descriptions may not be suitable for managers who desire new career directions. Job descriptions may be too rigid and cause decision makers to reject your experience because it does not compliment the current needs of the organization. A summary of qualifications is an excellent way of presenting skills and abilities that go beyond a job description. If you do not have direct sales experience, you may still list the ability open new accounts because you are indicating a potential, not actual experience.

CORPORATE MISSIONS MAKE FOR BETTER INTERVIEWS

A crucial element in running a successful business is the corporate philosophy because it guides the diverse operations of the firm while promoting corporate cohesiveness. Victor Frankl suggested success cannot be pursued. Success is considered the unintended side effect of one's personal dedication to a cause greater than oneself. This is precisely the function of the corporate mission. The corporate philosophy allows the various departments and affiliated personnel to see a common raison d'etre for the business. Anthropomorphizing the corporation facilitates camaraderie and facilitates conformity in decision making through group "identity." Understanding and complimenting a company's corporate mission makes for a better interview.

Effective mission statements include target audiences, statements of values, competitive strategies, statements of vision, general purpose and any remaining information to guide the business and inspire the organization for years to come. Mission statements are not only assets to the organization they can be insightful for job candidates wishing to obtain offers.

Frito-Lay prides itself in posting a 99.5% service level. Approaching Frito-Lay for a job necessitates underscoring a commitment to service for an interview to demonstrate elevated congruence and receptivity. Compatible experience is not as important as presenting viable ideas for increasing service levels.

By starting discussions on common ground cooperation and rapport is maximized. The first impression provides the foundation upon which subsequent impressions are interpreted. Consider the vision of Ford Motor Company, "To become the world's leading consumer company for automotive products and services."

IMITATION IS THE HIGHEST FORM OF FLATTERY

Bandura and Walters established social modeling theories to show how behavior is vicariously adopted by watching others obtain reinforcement. If hard work results in a promotion, more employees adopt a similar work style to get ahead. Companies expect employees and new hires to imitate the zeitgeist of the organization. Imitation has become so prevalent with some organizations books have been written about it. Men in Gray Flannel Suits, was a book illustrating the mandatory business uniform of IBM sales representatives. You could easily pick an IBM representative from the crowd because they all looked and acted alike. To this day you can generally spot a sales person by their tan slacks and blue sport coat showing the power of modeling. Thomas Watson believed clients would come to associate the look with the quality of service. If you wanted to land a job with the organization, you dressed the part. John Kenneth Galbraith observed the power of conformity when he stated a degree from Harvard in economics necessitated support for supply-side Keynesian theory or a post-graduate degree in economics would never be awarded.

Imitation minimizes resistance. By wearing attire compatible with executives already on board job candidates will be perceived as team players requiring little adjustment to get in step with the rest of the organization. Fit is critical. As the old adage implies, "When in Rome, do as the Romans." In psychology this process is called mirroring. It's in your best interest to familiarize yourself with the trade magazines executives read so as to show affiliation. Be ready to discuss relevant articles during the interview. If an article has been written on the company, or the firm publishes its own newsletter, find a way to obtain a copy. Like the above example with Frito Lay. How a company feels about its customers is excellent information for use during the interview. Any new products, plans for expansion, or awards are also excellent material for discussion. We live in an information age, and the more information at your disposal, the more value you can project to a company.

The internet has opened a new world of information at your disposal. Savvy job candidates minimize job competition by separating themselves from the job herd. Acquiring specific information about companies allows employer needs to be pinpointed for focused resumes and interviews. This approach is miles ahead of other shot gun approaches sending out a large number or resumes like casting a wide net into the sea of mediocrity. Resumes and interviews without focus lead to interrogations. Proactive interviewing anticipates company needs and strategically offers solutions for adding value.

FIGURE GROUND

Students taking Introductory Psychology learn how perceptions are biased and can easily be manipulated. In viewing the illustration above what did you initially see? Did you see two faces? Did you see a candlestick in the center? Did you only see the city? Perceptions are influenced by experience. Consider how employers are presented with a figure-ground opportunity when approached by job candidates seeking work. Companies represent the ground and job candidates represent figures. It is critical to be able to see both the figure and the ground to present an effective interview. Edgar Schein illustrated a natural conflict between the needs of the individual and the needs of the organization. Understanding how employees and employers have different needs is crucial to getting offers. Companies want to hear what is in it for them. They take the position they have compensation and benefits to offer worthy candidates. The objective is to encourage them to see your value as a compliment to their organizational by strategically presenting your skills and abilities as furthering their corporate mission objectives.

Resumes and interviews are opportunities to manipulate perception. Passive interviews place most emphasis on the needs of the job seeker and create a dominant response from the company. Dynamic interviews place greater emphasis on the corporate mission and encourage a cooperative response from the company. When resumes compliment the background of the company, job candidates are perceived as assets rather than liabilities. Job candidates unwittingly encourage defensive interviews by placing emphasis on prior work history instead of marketing future incentives. Experience is less motivating than incentives. Save discussions about your background as corroborating evidence for the incentives you offer. The emphasis is on what you can do for the company; not what you have done in the past.

In the illustration above, what do you perceive? An old woman! Can you see the young woman also? Leaving employer perceptions to chance is rarely in your best interest because you inevitably end up viewed as merely "one out of many." The psychologist, Maslow, called our tendency to stereotype "rubricizing." We group things into crude compartments (rubrics) because it simplifies thinking. Thought processes follow the path of least resistance. We generalize rather than see distinctions. Unfocused resumes and interviews are perceived as merely one of the many. Unique skills and abilities are quickly diminished when employers rubrisize because all job candidates begin to look alike. This is particularly true if several applicants are interviewed for the same position.

The goal of the job candidate is to by-pass employer's stereotypical perceptions by offering something different than the typical candidate. Few job candidates offer considered incentives. Would you hire a job candidate stating, "I am looking for a company that affords me professional growth," over a candidate stating, "I have several ideas for how you can achieve your mission objectives." Companies will give you what you want if you first promise to give them what they want. By investigating information about companies and their competitors, you are in an excellent position to develop insights into the problems and goals companies embrace. Such information is strategically portrayed in the resume and interview to create congruence, cooperation and rapport. Interpersonal persuasion necessitates job candidates look like insiders, not outsiders.

SELL BENEFITS

Passive dependent interview strategies present qualifications in unflattering, application style formats emphasizing the past. When most of the focus is on the resume, employer enthusiasm tends to be lower than when emphasis is on creative ideas emphasizing future benefits. Passive approaches are not as powerful as dynamic interviews emphasizing your knowledge and how your ideas complement the mission statement. Little comfort is afforded defending a resume being scrutinized under a microscope. Maneuver the conversation to the future. Instead of expressing, "This is what I did," confidently state, "This is what I can do for you." Inquire about the company's growth objectives while demonstrating how your ideas fit both short and long range objectives. The difference in interview tone is significant.

Imagine the job candidate who suggested doughnut holes as a way of moving more pastry products and increasing sales. Consider how a trial phase or part time employment incentives lowers obstacles associated with risk for consumers and companies. An interesting experiment involved political yard signs. If approval was given to install a small political sign in a yard, it was highly likely permission would be granted to install a larger sign a week later. Why? Because the law of cognitive dissonance shows people do not like to reverse earlier decisions! Similarly, if companies agree to part-time employment, it is likely they will be receptive to full-time opportunities in the near future. This is an excellent reason for job candidates to consider seeking part-time positions with the intent upon leveraging them into full-time positions down the road.

Candidates with no prior experience can land rewarding positions by marketing potentials attuned to the needs of the organization. Encourage employers to see opportunities rather than your background which leads to resume competition with other job seekers. Employers and people in general are motivated to fulfill personal needs and ambitions. When employers identify with their companies, they are motivated to hire job candidates who represent the fulfillment of corporate objectives. Psychology advocates undying interest in the problems facing employers as the quickest means to securing cooperation and rapport. Present your problem solving skills harmonized to the employer's self-interest and watch how offers suddenly materialize.

PUT YOURSELF ON THE EMPLOYER'S SIDE

Good companies create conduits of candidates. If you represent a fit for the company culture they will want to interview you even if no current openings are available. Look for opportunities to build relationships potentially paying off in the future. Many decision makers believe what you have done is the best indicator of what you will do. Therefore, decision makers are highly persuaded by evidence of achievements in your resume and during the interview. Be continually on the alert for ways you can help the company by offering solutions to a current problem, referring candidates for a specific job, or sharing a business idea. You will cement the relationship and mark yourself as a valuable job candidate they will remember and call when an opening occurs. Even the best companies have at least a five percent turnover so opportunities are continually surfacing.

Energetically approaching employers with solutions encourages "we against the problem" instead of "you against me" in an adversarial hiring relationship. Experienced business professionals emphasize content specific knowledge and transferable skills. Resumes highlight strengths. Interviews highlight your persuasive abilities. Be prepared to give specific examples demonstrating skill, personal strength and accomplishments. Become adept at converting organizational problems into solutions for other firms. The anthropologist, Marvin Harris, spoke of the first leaders as "Big Men" who labored hard in the service of others prior to asking them to unite behind a cause. When these helpers acquired sufficient following and work credit, their benefactors honored them with positions of rank. Leaders assume positions of responsibility because they are adept at identifying the needs of their followers. You can be perceived as a leader by first identifying the needs of the company and then volunteering benefits at the onset of the interview.

Candidates investigating problems facing employers are in stronger positions to formulate solutions as distinct qualifications over candidates who merely answer ads. Hit-and-miss approaches generally earn less. Like playing roulette, the ball spins and finally falls into a predetermined slot. The slot may be the door back onto the street or invitation to a dead-end job. Wise gamblers attempt to stack the odds in their favor. If a company needs sales and you present strategies for opening new accounts, you are seen as a solution instead of overhead. Companies pay well for solutions. They begrudge increasing payroll expense. Job candidates promising enhanced sales and productivity seldom walk away without offers.

THOUGHTS LEAD TO ACTIONS

Edmund Jacobson, conducted an experiment showing thoughts lead to actions. He wired subjects to a monitor and directed them to imagine running while he measured minute, electrical responses in their central nervous system. The impulses were compatible with running. His research was applied to athletes for improved performance through a process known as visualization. Another study divided basketball players into three groups; one group practiced every day; a second group barely practiced; and a third group visualized practicing every day. The group that showed the greatest improvement was the group that visualized every day. Consider the advantages of mentally rehearsing your presentation to employers for improved interview performance.

Like any professional sport or vocation, career advancement is a serious undertaking. A leading sales trainer confesses to spending an hour rehearsing in front of the mirror for every minute on stage. Webster defines the term "impromptu" to mean "without previous preparation." The goal is to rehearse to the point the interview looks impromptu. Rehearsing a handy arsenal of interview responses allows job candidates to present them in a relaxed, extemporaneous fashion. The decision maker will give you high points for what they consider quick thinking on your part. A chapter in this handbook is devoted to responses to interview questions that can serve as valuable tools in getting an offer.

Rehearsing reduces worry, self-doubt and interview resistance. Being passive during an interview encourages unpleasant dominance from the decision maker which will be discussed in greater detail in a subsequent chapter. Employers perceiving candidates as helpful tend to relax, are more open-minded, and are compelled to make offers. Background information about companies can be obtained from a variety of library sources as well as from informational interviews and friends. A list of resources included in the back of this handbook can easily be explored through online searches. Use them to identify companies and generate a list of incentives for employers. The key is to align with the company. Put yourself on the employer's side and watch how fast offers are proffered.

REVERSE PSYCHOLOGY

Messengers who communicated ill tidings in the ancient world were put to death. In modern times, the manner in which problems are discussed during the interview can be grounds for immediate disqualification. Reminding employers about high absenteeism invokes a negative knee jerk response. Suggesting you know ways to elevate employee retention invokes a positive response without negative bias. Encouraging employers to connect your solutions with their organizational ailments prevents you from being associated with the problem. It is preferable to be associated with a solution.

The famous ad marketing jingle, "Ring around the collar," created a problem in the mind of the consumer that a Wisk product promised to solve. Odor Eaters, Ban Deodorant, Dial Soap, Scope Mouthwash and a range of other products are sold using cognitive dissonance in a similar fashion. Life Alert was a product preying on the fear elderly fall and cannot get back up so they needed a button to press to call for emergency. These dissonant marketing strategies assume problems and potential problems want solutions. Problems evoke cognitive tension. Solutions give rise to cognitive relaxation. Just as products and services are successfully marketed through cognitive dissonance, job seekers learn to use reverse psychology to evoke consonance and alleviate dissonance. When your resume and interview convey solutions, consonance is elevated and job offers encouraged. According to the book, Contact the First Four Minutes, job candidates get approximately 240 seconds to make a favorable impression. It is risky business to use this precious time to set up dissonance when you might not be afforded the time to present the cure and end up falling on your sword. Use the time wisely by starting off with solutions and allowing the decision maker to associate your solutions with likely organizational problems.

Discussing low productivity is not as effective as discussing enhanced performance. The indirect approach ensures participation and cooperation. Successful problem solvers allow employers to elaborate on specific concerns while candidates assume the helpful role of facilitator. Developing proficient listening skills allows job candidates to formulate ideas on how they can lend assistance. Little is learned by talking. The management consultant, Edgar Schein, discussed the pitfalls of being an expert consultant versus a facilitator. When the consultant presents himself as an authority, the problem is handed to him. Little organizational support is provided to help him solve it. When the consultant markets himself as a facilitator, he teaches the company how to solve problems through participation and cooperation. This approach is predicated on the philosophy, "Leadership is best when the people say they did it themselves."

Consider applying Schein's approach to the interview. When job candidates present themselves as experts, interviewers pick their brains. When job candidates present themselves as facilitators, interviewers are encouraged to openly share their problems and goals. The more employers share, the stronger the rapport and the more information you acquire in addition to the extra time you acquire useful for coming up with solutions. A client made an excellent living selling Musak machines by approaching restaurants with research showing background music can increase food and alcohol consumption. Companies and employers receive ideas and reject invasions of privacy. "Let me help you" is powerful psychology because it emphasizes self-interest. Want to receive more offers? Enthusiastically encourage employers to discuss their problems so rapport is heightened. Subsequently market yourself as a process consultant while eliminating problems from your vocabulary. Let employers elaborate on problems while you elaborate on solutions.

START INTERVIEWS ON A POSITIVE NOTE

There is an anecdotal story of a farmer's high altitude apple crop becoming pitted by a hail prior to harvest. The farmer knew grocers would reject fruit with cosmetic defects so he made plans for filing bankruptcy. An innovator approached the farmer with an idea. Why not ship the apples with an informational note? The note explained the hail-pocked appearance of the fruit was proof the apples were grown at high altitude where sleet was common. Grocers knew their customers preferred the firm, crisp consistency of high altitude apples. The note was like an insurance policy and was so well received grocers quickly ordered the farmer's entire crop. Even though solutions are within reach, employers are often too close to the problem to see alternatives. Stating, "I know how you can ship those apples," is ten times stronger than, "I hear you are experiencing problems with your crop."

To start interviews on a positive note it is essential to begin each day on a positive note. Life is more about planting seeds than reaping a harvest. When the correct seeds are planted, opportunities for harvest are boundless. Life is more about creating you than finding you and an excellent way of creating you is through developing a skill for being of service. Every interview encounter represents a first step towards an interesting journey. The reason so many of us find it difficult to achieve happiness is because we fear tomorrow, resent today and believe the past was better than it actually was. Every interview is an experiment to find greater meaning and fulfillment. As Wayne Gretzky observed, we need to skate to where to puck will be not where it was. Being happy does not mean you are perfect. It means you are working on overcoming your imperfections. Learn to adapt to new circumstances and forget about trying to adapt the world to you. It does not work that way. There is no more encouraging fact than our ability to change the direction of our lives when we put our mind to it.

Lawrence Peterson

DIAMOND IN THE ROUGH

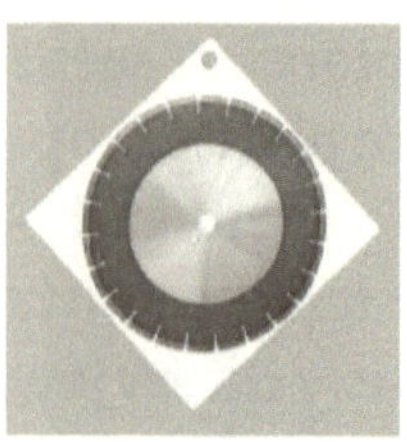

Career candidates resemble diamonds in the rough. A diamond begins as a hunk of coal. Under extreme pressure it is transformed into a rough diamond. The diamond becomes valuable once it is cut and polished. Despite the pressure of finding a job or a suitable career, the experience molds us into marketing machines capable of accepting a new cut and polish to transform our lives with exciting challenges.

Following the diamond analogy, a marketing designer called on an account with a major supplier of diamond tipped saw blades. The President and General Sales Manager requested an artistic rendering of a potential point of purchase display. The saw blades were mounted on square cardboard backings and displayed horizontally, like pictures on a wall. During the designer's initial needs assessment, the designer suspended one of the squares by its corner so it hung in the shape of a diamond. The two company officers were embarrassed they had overlooked the obvious merchandising approach. Many companies value job candidates with diverse work experience who can bring a fresh perspective to the operation. Your unique perspective is like a new cut on a diamond. Polish the skills presented in this handbook and watch your perceived value grow into lucrative job offers. Change is an indispensable facet of adaptation and growth. Although seemingly irritating at times, change is like a piece of coal becoming a diamond over time.

TRADE INSTEAD OF BEG

Traditional job search strategies approached employers passively as if looking for a hand out. A professional relationship implies a fair exchange of services avoiding unpleasant top dog, underdog relationships. Unwittingly marketing yourself as an expense instead of an asset conveys "taking" over "giving." Interpersonal psychology teaches givers gain and takers lose. Persuasion is reduced if the source exhibits personal gain. Persuasion is elevated when the source expresses views already held by the recipient. Psychological experiments show givers receive cooperation and rapport from others. Arrogance elicits aggression. Obsequious behavior elicits ugly dominance. Behaving like a passive doormat encourages employers to wipe their feet on you so if you do get an offer, it will be for low compensation. Why would employers respect a servile toady? Guarantee cooperation from Personnel Managers and key decision makers by offering a willingness to listen and a desire to be of service. IBM utilized a marketing approach based on informing the consumer how business machines could help enhance productivity. Once the customer became familiar with the benefits a rational decision generally resulted in a sale. Likewise, employers educated to the unique advantages in bringing you aboard will be persuaded to extend offers. Employers get sneak previews of future value when benefits are promoted at the onset of interviews. Movie theaters have traditionally used this approach for years to generate ticket sales.

A client launched an interior design company and quickly learned the importance of psychological incentives. Interviews began as informal walks through an owner's retail store. The designer subsequently asked permission to draw a reflected ceiling plan detailing the placement of fixtures and products. The designer returned with a modified design showing a better arrangement of fixtures and products. Like-items were arranged together. If a customer purchased hair coloring, shampoo and hair spray were within arm's reach. Consumer research showed customers tend to purchase at their eye height. Since the designer knew the average shopper was a female about 5' 4" in height, the highest profit merchandise was designated to a shelf 5" 2" from the floor and in the middle of the shelves where most purchases are made. The designer recommended placing heavily advertised merchandise at the back of the store so customers would walk past higher profit merchandise to get to the advertised bargains. The mere exposure to additional merchandise guaranteed additional sales. Since consumers are known to shop longer when exposed to unfamiliar music, new music selections were recommended to encourage additional sales.

Owners were impressed with the designer's renderings rationale behind the suggestions. The designer knew the application of consumer psychology to store layouts would elevate sales. To sweeten the incentive, the designer guaranteed store owners a 27% increase in overall volume or a speedy refund. The store owners readily accepted the offer and subsequently saw their sales increase by as much as 50% over prior sales. The more success clients posted, the more referrals grew. Incentives beat groveling for orders! The interior designer's reputation grew to the point his service was pre-sold prior to the interview. The designer practiced a simple troubleshooting philosophy with store owners, "You don't have to be sick to get better." He congratulated store owners on their business success and suggested his motive was to make their job easier. You don't have to work for yourself to employ a similar strategy. Approach any retail organization with similar incentives and you won't be turned away.

ADVANTAGE OF PRAEGNANZ

The notion of Praegnanz in Gestalt psychology suggests the brain sees whole objects before it perceives individual parts giving credence to decision makers making overall general impressions before looking deeper a job candidate's background and qualifications. We humans tend to order experience in a regular, orderly, symmetric, and simple manner. Praegnanz is a German word that directly translates to mean "pithiness" and implies the ideas of salience, conciseness and orderliness. Simply put, we take short cuts in observation and perceptions. Praegnanz involves several psychological laws. The Law of Similarity suggests objects will be perceptually grouped together if they are similar to one another. This law suggests job candidates will likely be considered insiders when they align their behavior consistent with the organization they are applying to.

Gestalt psychology differentiates two types of thinking: productive and reproductive. Productive thinking is involved when we experience an insight. This phenomenon takes place when we listen to a decision maker's organizational problems and subsequently see connections to other problems and solutions. For this reason, it is crucial to learn efficient listening skills so as to spot opportunities useful for making a favorable impression during the interview. Reproductive thinking involves solving a problem using prior experience. When we suggest we solved similar problems with former companies we are using reproductive thinking and suggesting we can solve the same problem again with other companies, thereby increasing our validity and voracity with the decision maker.

The expression, "paralysis of analysis" refers to the inability to make a decision because of an overemphasis on perfection. Perfect solutions are not necessary to project value to an organization. Watching a professional diver launch from a ten meter board looks easy until you understand thousands of hours went into training the central nervous system to make the feat look natural. Through introspection and rehearsing, job candidates can anticipate and cultivate effective answers to interview questions. The Law of Similarity suggests anything in our background that is close to a requirement could suffice in the mind of the interviewer. Anyone can learn to increase their interpersonal persuasion through practice.

It is a known fact the brain sees upside down. The mind corrects the picture so we see our environment in relation to gravity. An experiment was performed where a participant was required to wear glasses causing them to see the world upside down. Their brain quickly adjusted and they were able to function normally in an upside-down world. Our brains quickly learn to connect the dots to assist in adaptation. If the lines in the illustration at the beginning of this chapter were too far apart, like unfocused interviews, no perceptual connection would be made. It is critical the resume and interview make connections for employers. The connections only need to appear close for Praegnanz to be elicited. If your qualifications are strategically portrayed, the employer will connect the dots and see an opportunity. Since few job descriptions are exact carbon copies, the concept of Praegnanz means you background need only appear to be close to the requirements of the opening to get the job.

In the Escher drawing above, do you see geese and fish? Your first impulse is indicative of past learning. Like the illustration, employers can be persuaded to see diverse backgrounds as opportunities if properly presented. This is particularly important for job candidates changing career fields. You don't have to demonstrate an exact background. Interpersonal psychology teaches the earnest desire to help employers build better mousetraps is sufficient incentive to influence perceptions and persuade decision makers to make you part of the team. Forget feeling inadequate and stop shying away from opportunities because your background doesn't perfectly match the opening.

Unaware of what the job entailed, a client took a fact-finding approach to an interview for an Exhibit Designer's position. During his discussion with the owners he noted renderings of exhibits on the office wall. The owner was offering a starting salary too low for consideration so the candidate used the interview as an opportunity to pick the owner's brain for information. The renderings and information gleaned from the interview allowed the candidate to create a design portfolio prior to interviewing with a different exhibit manufacturer. Magazines provided ideas about products and provided a variety of renderings appealing to a varied clientele. Like the quasi triangle illustrated earlier, the exhibits only had to be close to elicit a connection with the employer's needs. An offer resulted because the company saw the potential for penetrating a new market. Information from one interview can be leveraged into an offer on the next. The close observation of little things can lead to bigger opportunities.

According to employment experts, the majority of employees are frustrated because their job descriptions require little creative effort. Nothing suggests quiet desperation like the inability to gain recognition through our contributions. Frustrated employees change jobs with greater frequency than happy employees. Normal corporate turnover is set at five percent although this number is rising because of rapid changes in the marketplace. Large turnover percentages should be scrutinized for problems with the corporate environment. On the employee side of the turnover equation, jobs typically held during a career is now approaching fifteen, with the majority of moves made after the age of forty-five. This phenomenon is partially due to the face older employees are beginning to realize many of the promises regarding their career are not materializing and they are not finding fulfillment in their jobs. Employment experts predict the employee of tomorrow will work less hours and occupy a variety of part-time positions to minimize the impact of unemployment. Currently, one-third of all positions are part-time and this number is growing because of change, higher insurance costs associated with full time, and workers who are unwilling to work evenings or on weekends.

Part-timers generally do not receive health benefits. Since two part-timers cost less than one full-timer, companies are beginning to minimize the traditional emphasis on job longevity. The single track career is rapidly giving way to multiple career tracks. We are seeing the advent of flex-time, the shortened work week, the wide-spread use of consultants, and a dramatic rise in home based job assignments. The trend away from granting tenure to teachers is a maneuver to shave costs. In the generic sense, tenure isn't in the worker's best interest because it frequently leads to reduced compensation. Why? Because employees are frequently taken for granted while their pay is based on what peers make instead of personal contribution. In psychology, this concept is referred to as habituation. You can enter a room and become painfully aware of the hum emanating from the overhead fluorescent lights. After you ears adjust the sound is no longer evident. Likewise, companies habituate to your achievements and take your contributions for granted. When companies quickly forget your last accomplishment and when you rapidly absorb your last raise habituation is in play. To ensure your accomplishments remain appreciated, change jobs for opportunities that represent growth.

CHANGE JOBS WHEN YOU ENCOUNTER THE FOLLOWING

When your review is delayed or slips into the next quarter.
When a new job title offers no additional compensation.
When too much emphasis is placed on promises of opportunity.
When "Good things are about to happen that cannot be discussed.
When your boss takes credit for your work.
When you are offered an opportunity to create your own niche.
When a small salary review is justified by your current salary.
When you put more into a job than you get back.
When you are assured of continued employment after a take-over.
When you get promoted to a job with a record for high turnover.
When you are transferred to the boon docks.
When you are asked to train others to replace your job.

Signs it is time to change jobs include a focus on what employees are doing wrong over what employees contribute; when companies place bureaucratic procedures ahead of a better way of doing things; when total emphasis is on cost cutting, profits and the singular pursuit of profit without consideration of the value of workers; and when politics, bullying, nepotism and cronyism lead to a toxic work environment.

Changing jobs can be refreshing and even returning to a company you have left can offer additional earning power. Companies offer former employees' raises over existing employees when they feel former employees have learned exceptional skills and abilities with another firm. Because of personnel department guidelines, loyal employees getting promoted from within frequently find their compensation routinely tied to other employees within the firm. Giving one employee a larger raise than coworkers causes political problems. Outstanding employees often become disillusioned because they get paid what lower contributing peers get paid. This is hardly an incentive to continue innovating. Returning employees frequently achieve larger compensation packages when their newly acquired experience with other firms promises additional benefits over the existing rank and file. Group dynamics shows employees justify less compensation when peers go along with the status quo. Forget justification and rationalization. Change jobs, learn new skills, and make more money!

INNOVATORS VERSUS MAINTAINERS

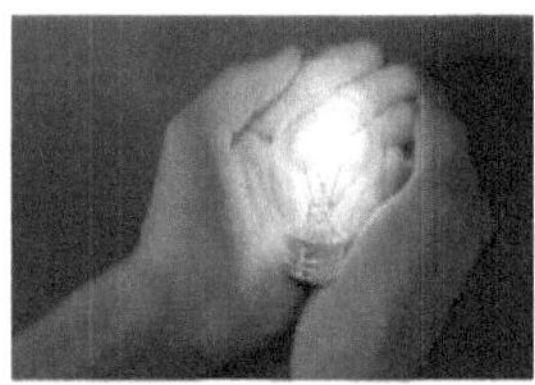

The classic research of Frederick Herzberg's Two Factor Theory illustrates factors affecting job attitudes. Factors were identified in the work environment causing satisfaction and dissatisfaction. Factors leading to dissatisfaction included company policy, supervision, work conditions and salary. Factors leading to satisfaction included achievement, recognition, responsibility and advancement.

Worker classifications can be conveniently separated into innovators and maintainers. Innovation is a primary requisite for new companies because systems must be created to achieve liftoff, similar to W. Rostow's economic notion of take-off. Organizations subsequently undergo an industrial life cycle, growing rapidly to a point of euphoria where an indomitable false sense of security sets in. During the euphoric phase companies frequently lower their guard making them ripe for takeovers. Innovators are generally paid more than maintainers. When companies enter into the maintenance phase the emphasis focuses on eliminating innovators to reduce payroll expense while elevating group conformity. Personnel departments gain tremendous power during the maintenance phase.

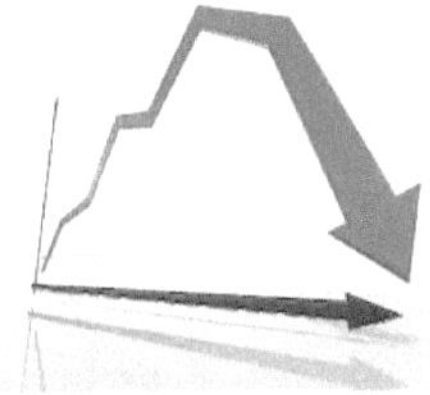

Max Weber wrote about the pitfalls of the maintenance organization. Once the idealists are gone, companies soon succumb to stagnation. Job candidates looking for work with stagnant companies will encounter highly entrenched personnel departments along with rigid job descriptions and dead end positions with an emphasis on strict rules and regulations. Stagnant organizations emphasize controlling costs and milking the system to get the greatest return on investment. Compensation becomes highly compressed. Accountants wax bold in the organizational hierarchy while policies and procedures become the driving force. Innovators who once received fame and glory for their creative efforts are now ridiculed, discounted and let go. If they are lucky they are given golden handshakes and replaced with custodians who will work for less because their job description lacks creative contribution. Statistics show companies placing greater emphasis on accountability (maintenance) fail in far greater numbers than companies who emphasize innovation (sales). In a rapidly changing economy, maintenance fails to take advantage of emerging markets and competition. This is precisely how the statement evolved, "Sales cures everything." Retail companies with strict payroll ceilings frequently lose potential business because customer service suffers. Rather than look for strategies for increasing sales, far too often the first impulse is to cut payroll. This can result in a negative spiral where the absence of customer service leads to further cuts in payroll until the business is shuttered. Savvy marketers understand customer service provides additional business opportunities with greater latitude for controlling expenses from the top down, not the bottom up.

A vending machine company performed an inventory assessment and found cokes were outselling other brands ten to one. The decision was made to stop stocking the other brands and only carry coke and sales subsequently suffered. From an inventory perspective the decision to limit product mix seemed understandable. From a customer convenience perspective, the alternate of choice was behind product sales. Despite selecting coke more frequently than other brands, the fact customers had a choice as to what product to purchase was sufficient motivation to buy a soft drink.

A sale is more important than cost control. This philosophy was confirmed by a siding company whose president suddenly passed away. The former president displayed a strong sales background. The newly hired president exhibited an accounting background. The accountant immediately initiated a cost reduction review and eliminated any expenses considered unnecessary. One such expense was to eliminate the annual customer fishing party taking place on a rented boat in the summer of each year. To the new president's surprise, sales immediately plummeted and the company was forced to consider bankruptcy. What the new president failed to realize was the interpersonal impact of the fishing party on sales revenue. Purchasing managers not only looked forward to the annual fishing party, they used it as forums for discussion. Companies can cut expenses to the point the company goes under. Wise job candidates understand companies need sales if they are to grow and prosper and gear their resumes and interviews in that direction. For companies to grow the emphasis must remain on getting orders. Excessive emphasis on cost cutting can kill the "goose that lays the golden egg."

As mentioned earlier, Peter Drucker suggested the future for American workers was in sales and marketing, not manufacturing. International companies and companies in third world countries need sales and marketing support if they are to grow their markets. The old adage, "Nothing moves until something is sold," is quite an accurate depiction of the importance of sales to overall company and global market growth. Understanding the importance of sales and marketing allows job candidates to leverage their background, qualifications and interests to the needs of emerging markets so their contributions are appreciated and their compensation grows.

IBM AND APPLE COMPUTERS

Innovation was behind IBM's first electromechanical bookkeeping system. The company subsequently coordinated creative efforts from Germany and Britain in conjunction with the United States to create the 360 mainframe computer boasting integrated circuitry circa 1965. The tail wagged the dog when IBM's microcomputer dominated mainframe sales twenty years later. Two men working in a garage demonstrated it didn't take millions of dollars to create a computer. Their company name, Apple, coined the term Personal Computer (PC) and became a legend in the computer world. Apple's sales aggressively took off, particularly when the Macintosh was introduced with graphics far superior to anything on the market. The innovative ideas of Apple founders Stephen Wozniak and Steven Jobs were soon eclipsed by the notions of professional money men who placed less emphasis on product innovation and more emphasis on marketing innovation as a means to increase sales and profits. The two original founders of Apple left the company. When Apple began to flounder, Steve Jobs was asked to return to the helm. The company soon reinvented itself through innovation leading to the current success of the iPhone and the iPad. The recent introduction of the touch screen cell phone has revolutionized the data industry. Other innovations are on the horizon offering additional career opportunities. Google is introducing computer glasses. Soon holographic displays will become commonplace.

Technological advances are indicative of Intel and their chipset finding their way into retail, energy, transportation, healthcare and education. Retail applications involve shipping and receiving, loading dock processing and computerized check out machines. Other areas supported by Intel include Banking ATM's, Wireless transactional devices, self-service touch display kiosks, vending machines, supply chain management, point of purchase terminals and ticketing machines. As the demands of a rapidly changing market continually change, chipset makers are pressured to come up with processors, software and miniature versions of former configurations to fit into ever smaller devices. Technical support has been vastly improved through remote monitoring. Online shipping has grown profoundly because of transactional software and devices. Business owners can now swipe a card using their phone to process credit cards. Chipsets, motherboards, and Ethernet products provide a wide array of job opportunities for candidates with backgrounds in science, research, development, design, management, marketing, website development, and sales. The information age will continue offer career growth for decades to come.

FIND COMPANIES COMMITTED TO GROWTH

The market is continually changing to address consumer demands. On the one hand, mass production and standardization is giving way to short production runs and tremendous diversity due to new technology. On the other hand, standardization allows for competitive pricing. Who could have predicted a digital watch or pocket calculator would sell for as little as two dollars. Thousands of specialized online magazines, newsletters and blogs are capturing their own following while traditional printed publications fall on the way side because they have become obsolete. ARM's BlackBerry, once dominant in smartphone markets, is losing marketing share to Apple, Google and makers of Android phones because they did not keep abreast with innovation. What company can expect to remain vital unless is continually innovates?

If you desire to make more money and minimize competition for really good jobs, market yourself as an innovator looking for unsolved challenges. Stay away from traditional companies reflecting high turnover, marginal growth patterns and no plans for new products. The key is to learn to identify company's committed innovative products and services. The average job candidate fails to discriminate between opportunities and in merely looking for a position accepts the yoke of mediocrity. Boredom and frustration soon sets in making the job a drudge. The majority of workers are underemployed and dissatisfied because their contribution and compensation is limited. The limitation began when they accepted an offer that either was not the right fit for their personality and interest, or was designed as a perfunctory work behavior.

Understanding corporate cultures saves wasted time and effort. A bright engineer was terminated from a truck company because his suggestions failed to generate enthusiasm with upper management. He saw inefficiency everywhere but his cost-saving innovations were continually snubbed as being the wrong fit for the company. During the exit interview he was informed the company was about to close. What they had been wanting was an Industrial Engineer who would come up with "quick and dirty" band aid fixes to keep production going. Because the engineer was not informed of the impending plant closure, his innovations were considered too costly despite demonstrating an attractive two year payback. Small wonder innovative projects were discouraged. Once the engineer understood he was hired for a temporary position with a company soon to be shuttered, he fully realized why he encountered opposition to his ideas. The engineer took a job incompatible with his background and expertise in innovation. Had the engineer done a bit more research about the company prior to accepting the position, the circumstances would have been dramatically different; either the engineer would have continued to look for a better opportunity or the engineer would have adapted to the short term fixes production demanded.

On a positive note, the engineer realized the misstep and subsequently found a company undergoing growth. Overnight the engineer's contributions were appreciated.
There are four questions to ask prior to seeking and accepting employment. Does the job pay what you want? Does the job teach valuable new skills? Does the job allow for networking with staff members who will help further your career? Will the job open larger doors in the future because of the company's ex-

cellent reputation? Any of the four considerations can provide justification for accepting a job. Dream jobs reward workers for their efforts for doing what they love. Working on problems you care about is far better than merely putting in hours to get a paycheck. Dream jobs open rewarding career paths. Dream jobs inspire you to higher levels of commitment and contribution. Dream jobs bring you closer to the people you like and admire. Dram jobs pay well for your efforts. Dream jobs foster self-confidence and self-esteem. Dream jobs challenge you to grow so you can fulfill your potential.

Many dream jobs can be found by contacting the decision makers directly. There are numerous resources at your disposal. LinkedIn, Zoominfo and job boards are readily accessible online. Creating a newsletter, website or answering questions posed on Google are good sources for job openings. Job fairs, networking, job clubs, emails and advertised openings are also valuable areas you will want to exploit. You will certainly want to consider a direct mail approach with letter of introduction conveying innovate solutions you have developed to help specific companies overcome their operational and organizational problems. Answering an ad is an invitation to fit into an existing job. The direct mail approach allows for greater flexibility in creating a dream job.

OVERCOMING JOB MARKET MYTHS

The fastest way to turn a mistake into a triumph is to change your viewpoint.

RATIONALIZING CHANGES NOTHING

Rationalization is a Freudian term illustrating how we attempt to make a thing seem reasonable when otherwise it is seen as irrational. Rationalizations contribute to ongoing and future career failure. Job candidates who do not understand the rules of marketing often believe there is a scarcity of available jobs when in reality new job opportunities are opening every day if you know where to look for them. Job candidates frequently believe employers demand exact qualifications; a degree is essential, and other job candidates are smarter than they are. Statistics show the best qualified candidates are not necessarily getting offers. Job candidates who can best project their skills and abilities as a solution to a company's problems are the ones first in line when it comes to a hiring decision. When job candidates rationalize, they tend to cover-up illogical acts or ideas. Not getting an offer is covered-up by blaming the employer or company instead of a lack in job marketing skill. A proactive approach is to develop greater interpersonal persuasion rather than denigrate others for a lack of success.

Multiply the number of want ads in newspapers by ten and you still haven't scratched the surface of available jobs on a given day because the majority of opportunities are not advertised. Published positions are invitations to get in a long line with other candidates. Certainly looking for work in a dying or stagnant sector is counter-productive. The fastest declining occupations involve electronic assembly, farming, stenography, sewing, telephone installation, textile and packaging assignments. Why? Simply put, robots with artificial intelligence are rapidly replacing these job descriptions. The largest job growth over the next few decades is expected to be in nursing, computer programming, computer systems analysis, electrical engineering, waitressing, and corrections. Although the majority of women are involved in waitressing, telephone operating, nursing, dental assisting, data entry, child care and library science, their acceptance into traditionally male occupations is rapidly increasing. Greater numbers of women are landing jobs as pilots, doctors, correction officers, computer programmers and politicians.

A recent survey of human relations experts predicts almost half of companies will hire contract or temporary workers in 2013. Temporary jobs are playing an increasingly important future in economic recovery. Where in the fifties less than one-eighth of the workforce was employed in information-oriented jobs, well over half of all positions today are of the information type. It is estimated over fifteen million new jobs will be coming on board by 2015 because of the new Cloud Computing technology. Apple has created or supported over half a million jobs to the U.S. economy and this trend is growing. Spin off jobs include truck driving, manufacturing, FedEx, UPS and application development. Over 24 billion downloads of applications have occurred over the last four years. Other information related companies also offer opportunities for job candidates.

Forbes magazine recently listed ten hot careers for the future; information technology rates high on the list because companies want to expand their IT departments. Health care professionals are in high demand because of the large number of "baby boomers" requiring additional health care services. The growing number of health care professionals requires health care mangers and support staff related to finance, marketing and human resources. Civil engineering is a career field worth investigating as the decaying infrastructure of bridges and highways demands revitalization. Life sciences and biotechnology is expected to see a forty percent jump in job openings through 2018. A growing number of companies are stating they cannot find qualified sales people to promote their products and services. Accounting and finance will continue to offer opportunities and over fifty percent of companies surveyed said they would hire more accountants if they could find them.

Computer literacy is no longer a hobby, it is a necessity, and this requisite will continue to grow as we usher in the twenty-first century. Since we are in the middle of an information explosion, job candidates are expected to demonstrate proficiency with several computer programs. It is wise to have a basic understanding of word-processing, spread sheets, presentation software, accounting software and website development. Long, tedious hours on planes are now filled with employees working on reports and sales projections provided by their laptop computers. Because airplanes are offices in the sky, aircraft are adapting consoles for Wi-Fi and USB connections. Airlines are beginning to relax rules for using computers during takeoff and landing because their electronics are no longer considered a risk to flight systems.

Computers are also used in conjunction with controllers for radio control. Private investigation agencies and the government are looking for radio control operators to fly drones and surveillance aircraft. Farmers use surveillance aircraft to check on herds and crops. Who would have predicted radio control would become big industry and be responsible for the military hiring and training thousands of recruits in how to fly planes and helicopters? The world is changing and creative jobs are coming available with alarming speed. Consider advances in robotics regarding nanobots and their impact on medicine. Virtual physicians are becoming a reality. The need for designers and engineers in prosthetics is ever growing to replace lost limbs. Cloning is a viable career field to grow hybrid crops or even organs without worries of tissue rejection because they come from the patient's cells. Translators are in high demand to remove global barriers to communication affecting all areas of commerce. Even hydroponics and aquaponics are growing enterprises because food and fish can be grown locally for restaurants and grocers without expensive shipping fees.

LOCATING THE BEST JOBS

Where are the best Jobs likely to occur? Recent statistics show California lost the most jobs during the recession and a growing number of companies are still leaving California in favor of other states offering better tax rates. California is listed as number 48 as one of the worst tax states in the country and future tax increases are inevitable. When companies face higher payroll taxes, increases in insurance fees, unprecedented energy costs, excessive regulatory burdens, and what is considered an unfriendly business environment, employees seeking job opportunities would do well to consider relocation as a possible means for receiving job offers.

The best places for finding work in 2012 are considered Texas with five of its cities occupying the top 25 best places to work, according to Forbes Magazine. California occupied half of the bottom 10 spots to find work in the Forbes ranking. If seeking work in California, San Diego and San Francisco are considered the best prospects in the current economy. In tight job markets, employers use sites like Monster.com to get the word out about their companies to grow pools of potential applicants. Factors to be considered are the price of housing, medical facilities, education, and natural resources. As job candidates migrate from the west coast, the price of housing still presents the most dramatic obstacle. Overall, sectors offering the most job opportunities are software engineering, financial planning, occupational therapy, web development and statistics.

A client displaying a background in finance admitted his job search was unproductive. When asked how he marketed himself, he confided his search was restricted to Fortune 500 companies. Since large companies can receive over a quarter of a million resumes each year, his resume, though impressive, was but one of many. The largest growth in the economic sector is in service related companies with 500 employees or less. He was encouraged to seek out local opportunities with smaller companies who receive fewer resumes. Within three weeks he landed a lucrative opportunity paying more than his previous position. Large companies often do not pay handsomely because they have standardized procedures and calculated compensation. Consider two kinds of openings, those advertised and those created when companies are approached with attractive incentives. "I can't find competent personnel willing to contribute to the momentum of my organization," complains the CEO of a Fortune 100 company. Therefore, when he hires, he assumes a defensive posture, offering candidates minimum compensation until they prove themselves. How long before candidates demonstrate their competence and loyalty? Only a Tarot Card reader knows! Candidates generally respond to low starting wages by putting forth minimum effort. It is not a win-win relationship when companies pay just enough to keep employees from quitting and employees work just hard enough to keep from getting terminated. Since over ninety-eight percent of job candidates approach companies without strategic incentives, firms insulate themselves by offering new-hires perfunctory job descriptions with minimal compensation packages.

Why volunteer to be underutilized and underpaid? Maintainers occupy dead-end jobs, are taken for granted, and receive marginal pay. Maintenance-oriented positions are often selected by companies because employees can be juggled or replaced when burn out occurs. Innovators negotiate better job descriptions and higher compensation accordingly since their skills and abilities are unique commodities. Which would you rather be? The best companies and the most interesting jobs involve innovation. Therefore, the task at hand is to identify a growing company committed to improvement.

Innovators are always looking for new, better and more efficient ways to facilitate growth and adaptation. Inventors, engineers, entrepreneurs, consultants and CEO's are generally considered innovators. The majority of workers and job descriptions involve Maintainers who are steady, practical and dependable workers but who generally change only when given sufficient cause or reason. The problem with maintainers is they frequently oppose change. When you consider the needs of the modern market economy demands rapid change, conflicts are unavoidable as the workforce begins a transition from maintenance to innovation.

Company's must continually innovate and must seek out innovative personnel to remain efficient, productive, ensure quality, and guarantee competitive positioning of their products in the marketplace. If seeking an innovative job, use words like invent, install, institute, launch, pioneer, present, unveil and establish in your resume, cover letter and interview. If seeking a maintenance position use words like conserve, continue, control, nurture, preserve, protect, repair, retain, save, uphold and sustain in your resume, cover letter and interview presentation.

NO SUCH THING
AS EXACT
QUALIFICATIONS

The dictionary defines "qualification" as a "skill or quality that fits a person for a job or position." In life we are confronted with possibilities and probabilities. It is possible companies will find and hire candidates exactly matching their qualifications. Frequently what companies consider the ideal candidate is someone already on board. Sly human relations department use the qualifications of existing employees as templates for future opening. As stated earlier, an advertised opening does not always mean an opportunity when an existing employee has been groomed for a job. In this case an advertised opening is merely a ploy where applicants are interviewed to satisfy EOE requirements.

Advertisements are more a reflection of the people who write them than the actual employment opportunity. Personnel drones are typically delegated the responsibility. Since few courses are offered in ad writing, the typical resource is an abridged copy of a written job description, if available! If not, copies of competitive advertisements found in the newspaper may be used. If all else fails, the department needing the candidate is asked to supply a laundry list of preferred requirements from which to create an ad. When this occurs, personnel departments generally use a job description of an existing employee. Since existing employees have company specific job experience, ads sometimes post proprietary qualifications that could only be obtained by working for the company. When this occurs, savvy job candidates understand the company prefers to hire from within.

Learning to read ads is very important to minimize unproductive interviews. Ads written to challenge the job candidate are looking for a specific kind of employee. For example, "5 professionals wanted who desire lots of money and are not willing to take No for an answer," is a typical ad for a commission sales job whose only prerequisite is generally a warm body able to knock on doors. Reading advertisements to determine qualifications also requires an understanding of the jargon. Lacking specific job experience does not mean you are not qualified to interview for a job opening. Jobs are rarely perfect fits unless companies are looking to hire from within or seeking a clone for an existing employee. Qualifications are tentative hypothesis. Over eighty percent of all jobs require basic skills only. Ads sometimes list minimum requirements i.e., an engineering license. Forget applying for the job if you lack the appropriate license. Ads stating an engineering degree is "preferred" are a completely different matter. If your experience is comparable to an engineering degree, do not be discouraged. Preferred translates into "would like better" and is far different than a minimum requirement.

When job candidates become adept at reading advertisements they quickly gain insight into the duties associated with particular career slots. Industrial engineers are people who figure out how to make things better. Emphasis is on finding ways to make things faster, safer and easier so companies become more efficient and profitable. Experience in production, machines, materials, information and energy are all excellent backgrounds for securing a position as an industrial engineer. Management control to aid in financial planning, cost analysis and production planning can substitute for degree requirements. If you know what the typical requirements are for a job, go to the library and familiarize yourself with the prevailing job requisites so you can customize your list of qualifications. Qualifications are not necessarily predicated on experience. There are several ways of addressing ad requirements in a resume. Regarding Manufacturing Resource Planning, "Am familiar with MRP" is one way to present a qualification. "Possess or demonstrate working knowledge of MRP" is another.

Ads continually appearing in the classifieds suggest high turnover. If the turnover rate is high, what qualities they are looking for in a candidate? Perhaps unrealistic expectations are responsible for employees quitting the company or being asked to leave. Another possible scenario involves a toxic working environment. Excellent opportunities exist when positions become available when employees are promoted to positions of higher responsibility. Asking how long a position has been open is an excellent way to determine how quickly a company needs a replacement. Companies not needing an immediate replacement tend to scrutinize backgrounds more closely to compare and contrast potential employees. This translates into a delayed hiring decision and an important consideration to be factored into your job search strategy. Leaning when a company expects to make a hiring decision keeps you from remaining on hold for a job that may never materialize or time lost looking for other, more immediate opportunities.

Approach ads from a creative stance by pointing out the benefits you will bring to the firm. If the company appears to be looking for a clone of the prior employee, ask for a little background information about the former employee so you can show congruity with the job requirements while referring to your skills and abilities. The more information you have about a predecessor, the better you can arrange your unique skills and abilities as incentives. There are a variety of questions to obtain information about the prior employee. For example, "Why is the position available?" Again, determining if the prior employee was promoted or terminated is valuable data when negotiating for the position. "What is the turnover rate for the position?" gives clues as to future opportunity and potential expectations the company harbors about the position. When your qualifications are attractive, watch how quickly a company stops using the last employee as a reference point.

IDEAS SUBSTITUTE FOR EDUCATION AND EXPERIENCE

Companies are bottom-line oriented and nothing affects profits like fresh incentives. Education can be an attractive incentive for firms because education and experience indicate a potential for solving problems. When job candidates possess relevant experience, education becomes less of a requirement. Although education is an important asset in a job candidate's arsenal, school attendance can represent a significant loss in revenue, particularly if class attendance conflicts with your work schedule. Before dropping a lucrative job to go back to school, consider your options carefully. Secure a catalogue from a local university and look over the course descriptions. Consider your work experience in relation to what is being taught in the various programs. Many business professionals have the equivalent of an MBA although they have never gone to graduate school. The rules of finance and management can be learned through practical experience. If you already possess a successful track record, do not mitigate your contribution to potential companies because you lack a degree.

Schools and universities are acknowledging there are many ways to gain information and training which is why many are not offering college credit for life experience. Be advised famous college dropouts include Bill Gates, Mark Zuckerberg and Steve Jobs who all became billionaires. As a substitute for a college degree there are numerous certification programs that provide expertise for different career slots. Consider certificates in paralegal, project management, real estate, information technology, computer repair, digital and graphic design, and video game design.

Substitutes for Education

If lacking a degree and the company emphasizes academics, you can enroll in a degree program. Even though the first class has not been attended, college enrollment demonstrates initiative. Employers give high marks for enterprise. Several fast-track, accredited degree programs are illustrated in Bear's Guide on How to Get the Degree You Want. Many degrees are offered entirely through correspondence. Colleges are quickly realizing a significant portion of their revenue comes from adults seeking higher educational credentials. Through necessity, night school has become a highly visible option for working professionals. The University of the State of New York offers credit for classes taken at other institutions, thereby bypassing the rigid residence requirements posted by many schools. You simply take the course at a school of your choice and have your transcript forwarded to the university. Once sufficient credit has accumulated, an accredited degree is awarded. Numerous degree programs from major colleges and universities are now offered online in a wide array of disciplines.

Accreditation is something to look for in a college or university. Basically, there are five regional accrediting boards in the United States. School accreditation means you have a degree from a school that not only maintains rigid standards of excellence, but these standards are also continually audited to ensure conformance with regional requirements. It also denotes your credits will generally transfer to other accredited institutions within the United States. John Bear also lists degree mills to consider avoiding.

Sales positions require job candidates show their selling skills in overcoming objections. A client interviewed for a position with a large insurance company preferring a bachelor's degree in their advertisement. During the interview the client was asked if he had a degree. The client responded, "I have something better than a degree; a proven track record for opening and servicing accounts." The interviewer was taken aback and reiterated the company made it a practice to hire only degreed candidates. The client responded, "Isn't it true insurance sales are made by individuals who can perform effective customer needs assessments so appropriate insurance programs can be recommended?" The interviewer agreed. "Isn't it also true a college degree does not automatically equate to an ability to open accounts?" The interviewer assented. "My past experience clearly indicates I can secure new accounts, maintain excellent account retention, and obtain referrals from satisfied customers. I have never been asked by a customer if I had a degree. Under these circumstances, I believe it is in your company's best interest consider my proven track record in lieu of your educational preference. I am confident you will not regret your decision." As you would expect, the candidate got the job.

Lawrence Peterson

DIRECT MARKETING WORKS

Typical job candidates go to the want ads as soon as a job is needed, ignoring the fact only a small percentage of high paying positions are landed in this fashion. Want ads do indicate potential openings. They also translate into long lines and stiff competition in a format similar to playing the roulette wheel, hoping your resume will land on the lucky number. Classified-oriented job candidates follow one another like lemmings down traditional paths of employment and jump off a cliff of obscurity into the sea of mediocrity. Other avenues are available paying higher returns on investment. If you possess a critical skill learned at one company, competitive companies are the first places to approach. Less direct approaches include initiating a research project needing input from leading decision maker. Offers can result when decision makers realize you have understanding of their product are sincerely interested in adding to the bottom line. Such approaches yield information about potential job opportunities.

Consider entering a program at the local college and electing to write a paper on a subject valuable to local businesses. This approach encourages interviews with local decision makers where you can show off your persuasion skills while gathering information useful for both the paper and employment. Write down several insightful questions prior to the interview, and during the interview you take notes to show interest. Human nature suggests most decision makers like to talk about themselves and their accomplishments. By establishing rapport, you encourage offers. If the question arises as to what you are currently doing, suggest you are investigating the field for potential career opportunities. If really ambitious, you can write a paper based on your research findings and use it as an introduction to other companies. Perhaps you discovered some unique means for marketing products. Why wouldn't other companies be interested in such information? They might hire you to implement such a program. Consider the job candidate who got the job by suggesting to a paper bag company the idea they could ship their paper bags in a larger paper bag and eliminate the use of expensive boxes or unsightly string.

A client went on several fact finding interviews with well-known psychologists for background information on a book they were writing. During the interviews the client was invariably approached with offers to collaborate on books the psychologists had long considered. In this instance, the client's direct marketing approach led to opportunities rarely considered by most job candidates. Such opportunities frequently arise from the mere excuse for an interview. Frequently, the journey exposes additional opportunities for collaboration because others want to be involved in similar pursuits. A few days of judicious online research promises to yield a plethora of information about products and services you can turn into informational interviews. Robotics is a hot commodity for manufacturing. The benefits of automation are obvious to most companies. If you have ideas on how a company can automate its operation for improved productivity and reduced operating costs, Plant Managers will show interest and grant interviews. A resourceful interview includes recommendations for plant renovation, equipment justification and how products can reach wider audiences. One study showed how merely calling local businesses for product demonstrations yielded an eighty percent acceptance rate. After all, why would a company turn down a demonstration if the product or service was congruent with the company's needs?

Approaching companies directly and negotiating a job description based on potential benefits to the firm is another means to getting an offer. Since negotiated job descriptions are not set in concrete, compensation has not been established or limited. This approach necessitates you develop viable ideas for implementation. Chat rooms and business networking groups can provide rich information about problems facing companies in addition to solutions you might employ. Identifying problems facing companies may be as simple as driving by their shipping and receiving dock and watching trucks arrive and depart. How efficiently are products handled? Do trucks typically wait prior to being unloaded? Is freight being hand carried or transported using pallet jacks? Is freight staged on the loading dock ahead of time to expedite loading? Are conveyers being utilized? Is material being over handled because of bottlenecks? You would be surprised at what you can learn from a few minutes of observation.

Years ago a businessman frequented restaurants and made a habit of commenting on the service. After each meal Adams would write a detailed letter to the restaurant owner regarding service, housekeeping and the menu. Adams included suggestions to be implemented to improve overall service and sales. Many owners responded with thank you letters and requested interviews to discuss the suggestions in greater detail. Adams' approach was simple. Along with the letter he included a message suggesting if the observations were of any value, the company was encouraged to pay him whatever they felt the observations were worth. Interestingly, checks were routinely mailed. Because recommendations were relatively obvious, Adams became known as "Obvious Adams." Key to his success was approaching companies with benefit. Like other successful trouble-shooters, Adams could afford to give away a few ideas as good faith, and to demonstrate he knew what he was talking about.

THE MAGIC OF ROLEX

Identifying what benefits to sell is crucial to a successful marketing and sales program. The success of Rolex is based upon an understanding they do not sell watches. Rolex sells prestige and recognition. You cannot ask $5000 for a watch when a $3 digital performs the same chronological function. Rolex promises a different set of benefits to the consumer. You do not clasp a Rolex around your wrist for assembly line work. Similarly, you do not strap on a Timex if trying to convey financial success during an important sales demonstration. If you do not believe people are influenced by the little accessories you wear, think again. Those most impressed by wealth can tell you where you buy your shoes. Packaging is critical in forming positive impressions. Anyone selling Rolex watches understands how important it is to project wealth over economy.

Consider a different approach used by the Timex watch company. Timex watches are marketed as inexpensive, reliable timepieces. Timex customers possess vastly different needs and expectations than Rolex customers. John Cameron Swassey immortalized the durability of a Timex by coining the phrase, "Takes a licking and keeps on ticking." Rugged, dependable and solid are the benefits to be obtained in wearing a Timex watch. Although Rolex watches could be described using the same jargon, no one wants to associate a Rolex with its ability to withstand rugged abuse which is contrary to refinement.

In applying the preceding marketing principles to career development, there are companies who look for dependability and low employee investment. Like Timex watches, modest jobs are suitable for job candidate's security, not prestige. The licking these jobs offer is to slug it out in the trenches and see who can work the most overtime. Instead of telling time, you serve time by fulfilling demands of a mundane job description. Forget packaging when applying for low-paying jobs because a suit is rarely required. Upwardly mobile job candidates demand more from work than toil. Carefully consider the kind of company and the job you seek affiliation with. Every work sector projects a unique personality. A steel manufacturer is vastly different from a computer manufacturer. Innovative companies are looking for creative workers who thrive on loose structure. The days of "I owe my soul to the company store" are unfashionable and demeaning. Apply the magic of Rolex to your career by emphasizing the right kind of benefits. Instead of underscoring you are a hard worker who has never taken a sick day off, accentuate how your problem solving competence typically saved money while increasing productivity.

A colorful Personnel Manager for a major firm stated, "Companies are looking for a magic suppository to shoot up the tail end of a chronic organizational ailment. They already know what job candidates stand to receive from a hiring decision. Instead of appearing on the company's doorstep and filling out an application, candidates should take time to investigate what kind of consumer the company is, what it needs, and what kind of employee would best fit into the goals set forth in the mission statement. In short, the closer a candidate complements the specific needs of a company, the stronger the job prospects. Rolex fetches handsome prices for watches because consumer self-interest has been identified and exploited. Job candidates receive heightened compensation when employer self-interests are addressed and maneuvered. Getting to work on time is commendable but hardly unique. Telling an employer how to move plastic containers to save the company millions of dollars over cardboard shipping boxes will certainly get favorable attention. Forget talking about what school you graduated from and what companies you have worked for. Make your education and experience evident by virtue of the ideas you present.

The entire notion of luxury has been exploited, from cars to real estate, with persuasive marketing strategies. For customers of prestige products, the high price is itself an important purchase motivator. Similarly, job candidates have the status of their former position equated in terms of what salary they commanded. If their salary was high, their contribution is perceived as relatively strong. If their salary was low, their contribution is perceived as somewhat ordinary or pedestrian. Since personnel departments generally employ a range of compensation, where you fall within the range is indicative of how the company values your contribution and how persuasive you are in commanding higher income.

To command more job offers and higher compensation, job candidates must learn to become adept at sales. You cannot expect someone to offer you an offer if you are not convinced you are a valuable asset to a firm. Be clear about your career objectives so you do not come across as unfocused and confused. Overcome self-conscious anxiety by talking about contribution rather than talking about yourself which can come across as egotistical. Be passionate about what you can provide a company and rehearse effective responses to hypothetical interview questions. Look at every encounter as an opportunity to improve your interpersonal persuasion skills. Career fulfillment is a life long journey. What you glean from interviews can help you with subsequent encounters with key decision makers.

COMPENSATION IS RELATED TO NEEDS

The dictionary defines compensation as the state of being compensated with money or payment. In business, the greater the need the greater the compensation. A movie entitled, The Big Blue opened with a scene of a diver trapped in a ship during a routine salvage operation. A representative for the salvage company needed an immediate solution to save the trapped diver. Time was critical. The salvage company paid a deep dive specialist a significant amount of money to rescue the trapped diver. The deep dive specialist was so accustomed to diving without oxygen; he performed the rescue without scuba equipment. The situation is not unique. The greater the need, the greater the expected compensation for a timely solution.

Trouble-shooters are in high demand. Technicians familiar with a specific computer system can tell you over the phone how to get your system back on-line. The level of compensation is related to the importance of the need. Companies faced with deadlines will pay handsomely for your service. By understanding what companies require, you can arrange a list of potential solutions and receive higher compensation. Few people call a pest control representative as a matter of routine. They call pest control when being overrun by roaches and termites. When airlines do not have scheduled flights, companies pay significantly more for private flights to arrive at destinations because emergencies and deadlines are important. On a similar note, companies will pay more to meet deadlines so as to avoid fees associated with penalties. When job candidates show they can help companies meet deadlines, their compensation is expected to be greater than for employees who perform routine jobs.

Seek greater challenges and watch your value to companies go vertical. Consider how cyber-attacks are shutting down computers around the world. Solutions at preventing such attacks will find receptive ears and job openings with both private industry and the government. When companies are faced with imminent data loss, they pay handsomely for solutions to keep them secure. Each time a virus hits the internet; millions of dollars are made by companies and employees who work with encryption, firewalls and email security to prevent data loss or damage.

MASLOW'S HIERARCHY OF COMPENSATION

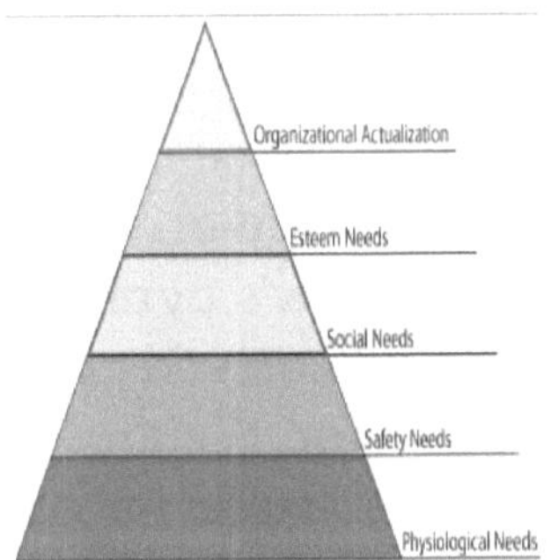

Maslow used a pyramid to show the hierarchy of human motivation. At the base were physiological needs associated with food, water, air and sleep. Higher needs included esteem and self- actualization. Although jobs offer to satisfy physiological needs to purchase groceries, toxic work environments can quickly sabotage needs for security. Safety needs include the desire for security, employment, health and family. Fear of losing security is the major reason candidates refuse to leave self-defeating working conditions, even when the situation threatens their physical and mental health. Maslow's theory suggests we cannot ascend to higher needs until we have satisfied lower ones. Dead end jobs and toxic work conditions thwart our natural need for recognition, acceptance, and appreciation. Esteem motivates candidates to seek upward mobility. Belonging encompasses the need for mutual respect, admiration and trust.

Maslow's hierarchy can be readily adapted to organizations with salary determinants. Job candidates who promise to help organizations satisfy higher organizational needs and are compensated at higher levels than candidates who work to satisfy lower organizational needs associated with security. When considering employment with a potential form, it is useful to apply the fundamentals of Maslow's hierarchy to the career potential of the offer. Does the job pay sufficient wages for you to purchase your basic needs? Does the job provide for job security, retirement benefits and a safe working environment? Does the job emphasize a team atmosphere with emphasis on a positive company mission?

Candidates who toil to get a paycheck are arrested at the base of the pyramid where low paid; maintenance-oriented job descriptions are prevalent. The top of Maslow's pyramid reside the innovators who desire respect, admiration and positive regard. Innovators assume the initiative for their own work efforts by continually making recommendations for enhanced performance and productivity. Interestingly, Maslow's hierarchy is frequently used in sales and marketing strategies. Clothing manufacturers' appeal to consumer' physiological needs by emphasizing their coats provide warmth and protection from hostile environments. Similarly, an expensive ski jacket can appeal to both physical needs for warmth and prestige needs for style.

WHY MOST OF US FAIL AT CAREER GROWTH

Change is difficult when people overestimate the value of what they have and underestimate the value of what they could achieve.

WHY WE RESIST CHANGE

Procrastination results from insecurity about outcomes. The familiar is clung to because change represents risk and uncertainty. Traditional career strategies are habits unexamined for their validity. One obstacle to growth is discounting prior accomplishments. Unless skills and abilities are recognized and inventoried, they cannot be presented effectively during the interview. Job candidates must be prepared to make positive connections from their experience to the needs of the next employer. Interviewing in a hit-and-miss fashion soon results in diminished bargaining power. Landing a meaningful job requires extensive rehearsal so your powers of persuasion are maximized.

Settling for less is a by-product of impatience and thoughtlessness. Filling out an application for a dead end job follows the path of least resistance. Job candidates passively accept the direction and control of the interviewer hoping a job offer will be forthcoming because they have not learned how to create value during the interview. Encourage change in your life by taking the time to cultivate marketing expertise and positive interpersonal dynamics leading to lucrative offers. Getting the right job is not a cake walk, where you walk around a circle and hope you are on the winning number when the music stops. Strategic marketing takes the guess work out of successful career development so you can buy your cake and eat it too. Be wary of who you confide in. Peer influence can hold you back. Your growth represents change and why would friends encourage you to grow if such a feat might potentially represent leaving them behind. Green eyed monsters prevent growth in others because they are afraid you might outshine them. Dare to experience the pain associated with growth. Look for new opportunities with other companies who will encourage you to master additional skills and abilities. The more you know, the greater your chances for mobility and compensation.

Change comes through a continuous struggle of thesis and antithesis resulting in a synthesis of goals, aspirations and experience rather than through inevitability. Every day represents an opportunity for change and with it a better life. In systems theory change is the inevitable byproduct of adaptation. The absence of change leads to obsolescence and stagnation. Change agents demonstrate a burning desire to improve the company and are frustrated at signs of inertia. Learning to embrace change is the prime directive of innovators seeking to help companies adapt to transitions in the global market. Words like conversion, development, modification, and reconstruction, are the vocabulary of change agents seeking to anticipate and capitalize on the needs of emerging markets. When we learn to accommodate, adapt and adjust to change we become reformers who help companies and organizations grow and regenerate.

Change agents take bold actions and are willing to accept the consequences when companies and employees push back. Becoming adept at proposing the benefits of change encourages personal and professional growth and provides validation of our efforts. With validation comes greater compensation and self-esteem. When faced with growth or stagnation, the choice is obvious. The difference between a mundane perfunctory job description and a dream job lies in our ability to spot opportunities and to capitalize on them through our understanding of marketing and interpersonal persuasion. Companies will happily cooperate when they see sufficient incentive to change. Your job as a change agent is to investigate and inform decision makers so they examine and consider alternatives that provide both you and the company a likely scenario for positive conclusions. Building a better mousetrap is counterproductive if the benefits cannot be sold. Become a student of observation and learn to package your observations as solutions and you will never have to worry about finding a work opportunity again. Although some companies may resist change, there will always be companies who are wise enough to understand change provides new products, more and better jobs, and global expansion.

Lawrence Peterson

CAREER PROGRESSION

The psychologist, William James, said there the only way to gauge an opportunity is by results. Career progression refers to upward movement and advancement. If your career is not progressing, try a new tactic. Job candidates limit themselves by paying lip service to change while rationalizing stagnation. How long would you continue to slam quarters into a coke machine failing to deliver a soft drink? Why frustrate yourself by knocking on unreceptive company doors who fail to make offers. Job seekers in the denial phase of their career religiously peruse the want ads and undergo one unreceptive interview after another until they begin thinking in terms of taking what they can get rather than what they deserve. Frustrated job candidates blame the system, the employer, the want ads, everything and anything except for their unproductive approach. Regression is the tendency to return to an earlier age. When job candidates continue in self-defeating searches, confidence and maturity suffers. When in between jobs, depression results from reduced or the absence of reinforcement from coworkers. Job candidates will generally feel helpless and depressed when they believe noting they do will change their circumstances. Career regression occurs when job candidates go into a fetal tuck and return to previous, less threatening positions. The problem is not a sudden lack of competence. The problem involves a lack of confidence leading to learned helplessness. Returning to a less threatening job might look attractive to someone in the clutches of doubt and depression, but regression serves to increase existing despair leading to a downward career spiral.

The psychologist, Marston illustrated how nature can reduce stress. The ocean and woods is pleasant to individuals experiencing emotional problems because the stimuli is overpowering, thereby shrinking our perception of our problems. The same goes for large corporations who can provide an overpowering sense of belonging to shrink individual identity problems and give a sense of purpose. Perspective is important to mental health. If experiencing career problems, finding larger problems to overcome will shrink current problems. Competition is reduced in direct relation to the size of the obstacles. Anyone can climb a modest hill. How many climbers attack Everest? An old Sufi metaphor suggests if you aim at an eagle, you may only hit a rock. If you aim at the sun, you may hit an eagle. Dare to set your sights on higher positions requiring more effort and growth. You will certainly achieve greater success using this approach than taking what you can get.

A track coach experienced problems with a pole-vaulter not living up to his athletic potential. The pole-vaulter faulted the equipment. The coach lowered to bar to five feet and asked the pole-vaulter to jump over it. The pole-vaulter thought it was a silly request but acquiesced and easily cleared the bar. The coach then raised the bar to twenty feet and asked the pole-vaulter to jump over it. The pole-vaulter's response was understandable. He balked at the new height, stating it was impossible. The coach then explained when the bar was ridiculously low all the pole-vaulter thought of was success. When the bar was elevated to twenty feet, all the pole-vaulter thought of was failure. Perspective and the courage to attempt new challenges are both important to growth. The higher an obstacle, the less competition will be encountered. By setting a lofty career goal and identifying the challenges associated with such a goal, job candidates will find fewer applicants seeking the same position.

An older job candidate lost their job and subsequently sent out hundreds of resumes seeking employment with another firm. Six months and several unreceptive interviews later relatives became concerned the job candidate was becoming desperate. Because the job candidate was approaching companies they did not want to work for, resentment was growing. After being encouraged to narrow the search to opportunities that piqued interest, the job candidate landed a job soon thereafter. Within one year the job candidate was promoted to the head of the department with a salary more than double what they were previously earning. A new found joy for work was realized and led to the development of a successful prototype. Unconscious resentment frequently arises when seeking uninteresting jobs. The number of interviews you go on is not as important as the quality of the interviews. You need only attend one carefully planned and choreographed interview to get an offer. Consider well each company prior to sending a resume or making a phone call. Do you like the product? Do you like the company? Is the opportunity interesting? Will the job appreciate your unique contributions? If not, find another career niche.

Approach avoidance conflicts

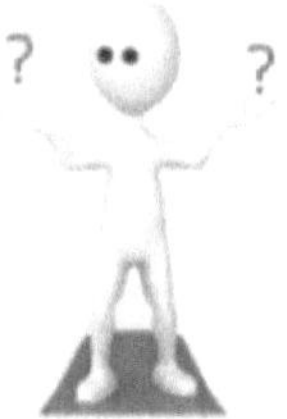

Career decisions represent opportunities for conflict. Kurt Lewin proposed a psychological model for intrapersonal conflicts. Approach-approach conflicts occur when a job seeker is confronted with choosing between two equally desirable outcomes. Taking a higher paying job requiring relocation is one example. Accepting a promotion at your current location without a pay increase is another example. Avoidance-avoidance conflicts occur when a single goal or desire represents conflicting negative outcomes making it difficult to choose the lesser of evils. Accepting a low paying job to make ends meet is a convenient example. Approach-avoidance conflicts result from a single goal or desire both desirable and undesirable. Accepting a management position forbidding fraternization with former coworkers is an example. When confronted with difficult choices, the greater the difficulty in making a decision, the higher the stress.

Take care in selecting the right company, position, and features. Some jobs require a great deal of overtime. Are you willing to work extra hours to get ahead? Other jobs require extended travel. Can you live in a hotel room for days at a time? What if the job requires relocation? Uprooting the family can be traumatic. Consider making a decision list by drawing a line down the center of a blank sheet of paper. On one side, list all the positive elements associated with a career decision. On the other side, list all of the negative elements associated with a career decision. The positive side should significantly outweigh the negative side if job satisfaction is to be realized and sustained. Once a company has been selected and an interview granted, do your homework. Just as you negotiate on finance charges when purchasing an automobile, compensation packages are also negotiable. You fantasize driving down the road in your new automobile prior to buying it. Think hard about the job description. Does it excite you or would it merely serve to make ends meet? Impulsive car selections translate into a great deal of post decisional stress. Think of the impact on your personal life when making an impulsive career decision!

We make scores of decisions unconsciously influenced by bias, emotions, reason, and memories. Job candidates must confront their decision making style to determine whether they are actually thinking or merely exercising memories. Frequently we give the past more positive weight because we fear the risk associated with tomorrow. When choices lead to greater well-being, we are on the right track. When our choices continually let us down, we need to reevaluate our approach to change and alter our behavior accordingly. All that we are is the result of what we think.

INTERVIEWS ARE 99% PSYCHOLOGICAL

Failure to get an offer does not necessarily mean you did something wrong. Failing to get offers generally means you failed to do something right. Dwelling on failure without identifying problems and developing solutions to change outcomes leads to reduced self-esteem and confidence. Rather than concentrate on potential inadequacies focus on what gets offers in the first place. It is a psychological fact business leaders are influenced by the media. Negative press encourages fear that translates into an economic recession. Poverty consciousness translates into an economic slowdown, thereby giving credence to a self-fulfilling prophecy.

Successful golf instructors will tell you fear of a water hazard translates into topping the ball into the water. The brain only hears WATER! It is preferable to concentrate on a desired landing spot, putting the water hazard out of your mind completely. The first shot in golf sets you up for the second. It is hard to play out of the trees or the rough. It is impossible to play out of a lake. Jack Nicholas has long advocated positive visualization prior to making every shot. The same goes for career development. The first impression during the interview is just as critical as the first shot into the fairway. Practice positive psychology and expect success, not failure. Focus on presenting benefits to the organization while eliminating personal needs from your mind altogether.

Berlyne discovered an important area at the base of the brain stem called the (RAS) reticular activating system. This area is responsible for stimulating arousal when presented with new or meaningful information. You can be in a room full of boisterous people and suddenly hear your name whispered on the other side of the room. Why? Few things are more meaningful to us than our name. Job candidates can take advantage of this process by discussing topics of interest to employers thereby guaranteeing their optimum arousal and rapport. Sales trainers have suggested agents use the buyer's name as many times as possible during the presentation because everyone likes to hear their name. Talking about your background is not as potent as discussing ideas for improving the company. Professional sales people offer incentives at the onset so the buyer sees a fair exchange of his money for the representative's product or service. So can you.

FRESH BAIT CATCHES FISH

Stale bait is never as inviting as a fresh, tantalizing lure. Successful anglers continually check their hooks to ensure the lure is in good working order. Fish may nibble stale bait. They rarely bite when their appetite is not aroused. Employers may grant interviews to look job candidates over. Employers are not likely to make offers when interviews are preoccupied with the past (stale bait) because the emphasis is on where you were not where you are going. Unemployed job candidates typically start off defending their past to show they still have worth to a potential employer. Similarly, candidates who defend their past may actually be communicating to a decision maker they have something to be ashamed of. Forget the past. Concentrate on the future and incentives increasing employer appetite. The stigma of unemployment is significantly minimized when the conversation moves to future incentives (fresh bait). Clearly state what you can do for the company while utilizing prior accomplishments with other companies as corroborating proof is necessary. Play up potential contributions to the immediate company and see how the conversation changes from an interrogation of what you have done to interest in what you can do. Discussing your past is static. Discussing the future is dynamic.

Past achievements, though impressive, may not be directly transferable to the new position. You don't want a nibble. You want a direct strike! Benefits are forward looking and arouse employer appetite. Move the conversation to the future and new ideas applicable to the company's growth. Ask where the company wants to be and what it wants to accomplish in the next five years. How will it attack the market and fend off competitors? Show how your experience complements future objectives and watch the employer immediately respond with interest.

Consider the weaver bird. Males work tirelessly in weaving a nest from grass to attract an eligible female. Strand by strand the male bird labors in hopes of impressing the discriminating gaze of the female. When done, the female lands on the side of the nest and takes her time inspecting its workmanship. If approving, she moves in and lays her eggs. If a nest is not immediately chosen, the nest quickly wilts and turns brown. Female weaver birds never select a stale, brown nest. The frustrated male must tear down the nest start over again, much like candidates who fail to impress decision makers on the interview. They must obtain new interviews and offer stronger incentives on the next go around. Fresh ideas, like nests of fresh grass, are better than stale accomplishments. Each interview takes energy, like building a new nest. Ensure you have done your homework and put forth the effort to persuade employers to consider your value so you minimize the number of interviews you attend prior to getting an offer.

A riddle once involved standing at a crossroad where two separate paths were guarded by two sentinels. One sentinel always told the truth. The other sentinel always told a lie. Travelers could ask but one question prior to embarking on one path or the other. What question would you ask? The riddle requires rephrasing the question into the future. The solution: "If I asked you tomorrow what was the correct path to take, what would you say?" Simply put, the guard who always tells the truth would still answer truthfully. The guard who always tells a lie would have to change his response, forcing the guard to indirectly tell the truth. This example illustrates the importance of placing emphasis on future benefits to evoke greater cooperation and rapport.

A job candidate went on an interview affording an excellent opportunity. The interview was moving along smoothly until the interviewer asked, "Why did you leave your last position?" The candidate panicked since the question was obviously loaded. The term "leaving" implies a problem. Should you find yourself in the same position, remember to move the conversation to the future. Forget discussing the lack of challenge with your last assignment. Discuss your need for greater problems to solve. New challenges suggest strength and avoid explaining prior conflicts which reduce marketing appeal. A productive response to the question above might be: "I have been fortunate to have worked with a number of successful executives who taught me the importance of problem solving competency. I solved the major problems with my last firm, and am seriously looking for new challenges with a company like yours so my competency can continue to grow."

THE POWER OF UNAVAILABILITY

Laboratory rats required to climb steep inclines to get their food sustained greater motivation in climbing the ramp once food was withdrawn than those conveniently presented with food on level ramps. The harder we work for something, the more we justify the effort. Our economy operates on the principle of supply and demand. Like diamonds, if the supply is restricted the price remains elevated. If the market were suddenly flooded with diamonds, the price would plummet. When our qualifications are considered in short supply, our value goes up. It is human nature to want what we do not have. Exclusive translates into higher cost. When companies think they are stealing you from another firm the tribal instincts take over. Unavailability translates into added worth and greater bargaining leverage when it comes to job opportunities and income.

It is a well-known fact headhunters want to work with candidates who are working, not those in between jobs. There is an unconscious bias working against unemployed persons by those who hold jobs. Unemployed candidates can expect companies to subject them to greater scrutiny than employed candidates. Part of the rational is to determine if the candidate is unemployed because of an underlying problem. One strategy for minimizing this unpleasant experience is to move the conversation from the past to the future. Ideas set a positive foundation for a good interview because they are forward-looking. A candidate operating as a service provider minimizes the stigma associated with unemployment. The relationship becomes "we against the problem," and makes for good psychology.

To minimize the stigma associated with being in between jobs, consider alternatives to remain employed. For example, there are volunteer positions that do not pay but are still considered employment. There are also part-time positions that may not pay high compensation but are still employment. You might find you prefer several part-time positions to a full time opportunity because of the added flexibility. There are also numerous self-employment opportunities that can fill in blanks on a resume while you seek a position with another firm. A recent law school graduate became an entrepreneur and walked dogs in Central Park to show employment while investigating other career opportunities. Although waking dogs might not look like the most ambitious undertaking, it does eliminate unemployment bias. Another consideration would be to start an Ebay company. Again, the emphasis is on reducing the bias associated with unemployment.

RAPPORT AND OFFERS

Be perceived as an insider by promising to contribute something of value to the firm instead of an outsider who surveys the terrain to claim a desk and title. The word, "You" emphasizes alienation. The word, "We" stresses team dynamics. The word, "Me," is the least meaningful of all. Strategies for developing rapport include making a positive first impression, mirroring body language, listening and asking pithy questions. Remember the interview is not actually about you, it is about the value you potentially bring to a firm.

When successful job candidates go on interviews they seldom inquire about available benefits, hours of work, or personal details about the job whatsoever. Such questions arouse employer suspicion about your work motives. Once the conversation turns to benefits, you have earmarked yourself as a security-oriented candidate volunteering for a mundane job description that pays less. Portray a refreshing change and express devoted interest in the challenge. You can always refuse an offer if the opportunity is not comparable to your level of skill and the difficulty of the job description. The main intention is to get the employer to perceive you as an insider and to ask, "When can you start?" They generally do. When you receive an offer you have an edge on other interviews with other companies because you have a bird in the hand, so to speak.

A Personnel Manger shared how a candidate responded when asked how many hours was considered appropriate to the job. The candidate stated, "As many as were required to get assignments done." The Personnel Manager liked the response and an offer was imminent until a gaff presented itself. The interviewer brought the interview to a close by asking the candidate if he had any additional questions. The job candidate made the mistake of inquiring about company benefits. The tone of the interview changed and the candidate was passed over. The best question is whether the position affords sufficient challenge to help you grow in competence so you can contribute more to the organization. No one likes to be a slave, but companies expect enthusiasm for work. Forget personal incentives until after an offer is made, unless the company wants to use them as part of a negotiation package. This usually means they want to offer you less money. Get the offer first and then discuss the benefits of the job package. Remember, there are no decisions to be made until an offer is tendered.

RUNNING THE CAREER SERVICE MAZE

Knowledge quickly turns the path of error into the path of truth

LAND JOBS FASTER

Personnel specialists now say it takes an average of two years to land another job. They are undoubtedly referring to candidates using traditional approaches to finding work. Projecting organizational incentives works like a strong magnet for attracting offers. Magnetism is based on the principle of internal alignment. Candidates attract offers when their behavior matches the internal expectations of the company. Looking for a convenient slot rarely results in the new job being any better than the last. Convenience comes in a distant second as the quickest means to getting an offer. It is an interpersonal fact the fastest way to get others interested in you is to first be interested in them. A magnetic personality implies the ability to attract others by appealing to their self-interest. Dale Carnegie created an institution on this concept. Attend a social gathering and do nothing more than listen to what others say. You will rapidly develop a reputation for being intelligent. People admire good listeners. Employers will volunteer inside information which can be reinforced to get an offer when they are encouraged to share how they got where they are, or what obstacles they had to overcome to move upward within the organization. To land jobs faster bring something of value to the bargaining table other than an open hand. The difference between lending a hand and an outstretched hand with the palm up is profound. Demonstrate sincere interest in the achievements of others and realize greater rapport and cooperation.

A job candidate trained in effective listening attended an interview for a sales position with a satellite communication company. After the introduction the job candidate encouraged the owner to share why he got into the business. While the owner was talking, the candidate nodded slowly to encourage more dialogue. The candidate used positive body language, occasionally looking up to the left to show he was thinking about what was said before asking an insightful question. With each question the candidate summarized and restated what the owner said to show he was listening. The way the candidate rephrased what the employer said demonstrated he knew a great deal about the communication field. The approach impressed the owner. "You seem to know a great deal about the field and I like the way you handle yourself," the owner said. "I would like you to seriously consider becoming a part of the team." Since the candidate had sales experience, the interview was indicative of the way customers would be handled. Since the decision maker believed an effective sales agent gets the customer talking, the candidate received high marks. When you think about it, career development means selling your skills and abilities.

Recent statistics suggest over fifty percent of the working population now work directly or indirectly for state and federal governments so considering career options with federal agencies makes more sense than ever. Opportunities exist in Alcohol, Tobacco and Firearms, Agricultural Research Service, Amtrak, Bureau of Prisons, Consumer Product Safety Commission, Customs and Border Patrol, Department of Education, Department of Energy and many more. The list is long and the government frequently hires in times during economic downturns. Considering usajobs.gov for federal jobs by state. Also review statejobs.com for state opportunities around the country. Usa.gov lists federal positions available in the various departments along with benefits. Consider taking the PACE government test to qualify for many government jobs not listed in advertisements.

ALL THAT GLITTERS TISN'T GOLD

Career maze strategies read like the title of the spaghetti western, "The Good, the Bad, and the Ugly." Although the numbers conclude the most effective means for securing work is to apply directly to an employer, this approach includes the millions who merely fill out an application for a minimum wage position. The second most frequently used approach is to ask friends. Third goes to the want ads. And the remaining candidates look to search firms, private employment agencies, state agencies, schools, the tooth fairy, etc. Any of these approaches can yield an employment opportunity. The difference in the quality and quality of the opportunity relies on your interpersonal skills.

Applications are mechanical screening devices created by Personnel Departments to standardize employees. Consider the following analogy: New home owners often find it necessary to prepare their yards prior to planting grass seeds. One way to accomplish this is to nail a screen on a primitive wood frame and sift the soil until only dirt is left. The size of the holes in the screen is an arbitrary decision. This is precisely the function Personnel Departments fulfill. The level of scrutiny candidates undergo is a unilateral decision. Anyone failing to pass through the holes in the screen is rejected. The end result is a homogenous group of workers who look and think alike. Physicists call this process atrophy, where energy seeks the lowest, uniform level resulting in organizational suicide. The lowest common denominator causes workers accept miniscule raises because everyone is in the same boat. The thought process is, "What makes me better than anyone else?" The end result! You end up discounting your skills and abilities and take what is meted out.

Although there is safety in numbers, career fulfillment along with higher compensation is generally associated with innovators, not maintainers. Job candidates would be well served to seek interviews outside of personnel departments with key decision makers so their resumes and letters of introduction get the attention they deserve. By doing a little research it is generally easy to find the names of department heads within given organizations and send a resume to them directly. If the resume is handed down, it has the weight of the higher office on its side. When resumes are handed up from personnel departments, it generally is one of many in a stack of potential job candidates. If you can bypass or eliminate the competition, you have a captive audience to pitch to persuade with your solutions. Since employers follow the path of least resistance, encouraging them to see your value is far easier when they do not have other candidates to consider. For this reason, many career experts encourage job candidates to approach companies directly rather than merely answer want ads.

THE CRONY APPROACH

Although job candidates get hired based upon the recommendation of others, this approach necessitates your friends are in a better position than you are and they can overcome their fear you might embarrass them once you are hired. Like sponsoring someone from another country - it sounds good until you find out you are responsible for taking care of them, even if they cannot find work. Mixing business with friendship can lead to problems. Further, friends can become distant or smug in giving advice when they find out you are temporarily unemployed. Finally, friends frequently cannot give objective advice when it is needed most. It is wise to consider the possibility friends might unconsciously want you to fail for several reasons. Friends might fear a job offer will necessitate you relocate. Also, friends might fear you will acquire a better position or greater compensation than they presently earn. Of course there is the unpleasant possibility your friends will seek your unemployed status as a weakness.

Now that the caveats have been discussed regarding recommendations from friends, it is important to point out quality referrals can help job candidate's open doors to work opportunities. One approach is to search for companies online and seek out contacts and networks who may be able to assist you. An employee, client, and vendor are excellent sources for referrals. Frequently job candidates use Facebook friends or LinkedIn connections for help with find a job. Consider using SimplyHired.com's, "Who Do I Know?" tool to see who you are connected with on LinkedIn and Facebook. The following is an example of a generic referral request letter.

Dear Referent:

I am a friend of Jane Doe and she encouraged me to forward my resume for your review. I worked with Jane Doe at the Desert Community Agency, where I was technical director. Together we worked on several local agency projects.

I am interested in relocating to the San Gabriel area in the near future and would appreciate any recommendations you might offer for conducting a job search, finding job leads, and any logistical information you can provide for relocating.

My resume is attached. Although most of my experience is in directing volunteer staff in theater design; I have also worked at prop design and theater renovation during my career.

Thank you for your consideration. I look forward to hearing from you.

EMPLOYMENT AGENCIES

Employment agencies frequently land jobs for the confused, insecure, and the apathetic. Ironically, employment representatives look through the same newspapers and trade magazines as everyone else. The difference is they make a phone call to the employer to obtain interviews for potential clients. It is emotionally easier to represent someone than to represent yourself, which is why employment representatives are able to project such courage in seeking interviews. If you feel the need to employ the services of an agency, why not start your own, making sure you are your first client. You only need to place one client to succeed.

You might be surprised at how many times the employment representative gets offered the job they are seeking to fill with one of their clients. Since employment agencies are paid by the person they place, they ask for a percentage of the job applicant's first year salary. Ouch. Some require advance fees with the promise of job appointments that frequently never materialize. They may offer to help you develop your career goals and to help you negotiate a lucrative offer that rarely if ever happens. Research shows successful candidates do not use agencies. Rather, they use networking, resumes and informational interviews to get offers.

A Personnel Manager with a large wholesale organization confided they use employment agencies to sift through applications for the best general fit. The employment agency then calls ten of the best candidates for a brief phone interview. Of the ten, four are set up for face-to-face interviews with the company. From the four the employment agency and the company narrow the choice to only two candidates from which to make a hiring decision. The final decision to hire is composed of several factors: experience, education, achievements, personality and salary expectation. Screening begins at the resume level. It is wise to spend extra time ensuring the resume is an effective marketing tool. A few examples of resumes that have landed job seekers jobs appears later in this handbook.

If you must use an employment agency, consider investigating any certifications they hold. Temporary agencies lime manpower.com are growing in popularity, despite low compensation and erratic hours. Temporary healthcare and nursing associations offer work assignments ranging from part-time to long-term care for recovery and hospice patients. Consider nursfinders.com and healthtempo.com when performing an online search in the nursing field. Employment agencies scoring the lowest reviews are those offering home employment opportunities which generally turn out to be a scam.

WANT ADS - CAVEAT EMPTOR

Applying to a classified ad or posted ads on job boards is considered passive dependent behavior because job candidates are merely responding to someone else's initiative, namely the person or company taking out the ad. The most used and abused media for finding work is undoubtedly the want ads. The positive aspect of classified openings is they often indicate a job prospect. The word "often" is used because want ads are also manipulative tools used by fee charging employment firms who advertise hypothetical openings to secure a list of potential clients. Search firms use the same ploy in an endeavor to talk disgruntled employees into leaving their present position for another, hoping they can earn double commission by getting your to change jobs and filling your former position. If the ad uses a Post Office Box, beware. Companies fearing blowback from labor unions or equal opportunity laws may advertise job openings when they already have a favorite candidate they expect to promote from within. If you have left an interview knowing you nailed it, but no offer was forthcoming, it might be you were used as filler by Personnel Departments required by companies to submit a minimum number of applicants. Although it is not possible to always determine a company's motives, it is wise to understand some of the tactics used by companies at your expense. In short, an advertised opening is not always an opportunity but always is designed for the benefit of the company posting the ad.

If in sales, what kinds of products and services are being offered? Beware of advertisements that pull at your ego. "Looking for power closers who need to make $5,000 a week!" Such ads are designed to attract high risk candidates willing to try anything once. The company throws the candidate into the field on commission and benefits from any sales made without paying a dime because you did not last that long. Subscription sales experience incredibly high turnover. If you are asked to attend an orientation meeting for a job, expect a room full of applicants companies expect to dupe into door to door sales. Remember, "There ain't no free lunch." One ad for a lighting company sought to attract sales representatives with the caption, "Last job." The same ad ran for over a year suggesting high turnover in the position. Read ads carefully and compare similarities in positions. A composite will soon surface you can use to determine the quality of an advertised opportunity.

With a little research, you will quickly get a pulse rate on available job openings. Many ads tell you what problems are facing specific industries by virtue of the qualifications requested. Personnel related positions may require EOE (Equal Opportunity Employment) familiarity, whereas transportation jobs necessitate DOT (Department of Transportation) proficiency. If you aren't familiar with a specific qualification, look it up. There are books devoted to regulations yielding a vast amount of valuable information. Understanding regulations helps convince companies of your knowledge in the field. Each occupational area has its own jargon and requirements. The intelligent researcher can tell much from comparing and contrasting advertisements. Do your homework and approach your job search as a career in itself. You can find jobs by city, state, company, industry and title as a start.

If after reviewing ads you find your background is not a convenient match, consider restating your background to become more congruent with available job openings or a new career track you find more appealing than your prior assignments. A background in design can be leveraged into exhibit design, landscape design, industrial design, store interior design, fire protection design, and manufacturing facilities design with a little homework and tweaking of your cover letter. The preceding examples provide overlap redundancy in job descriptions. The basic requirements for each respective job description are highly similar. Because of the current downturn in construction of homes, construction workers can still find viable opportunities in field involving alternate energy with wind farms, solar grids and the installation of solar powered water heaters.

A client with a background in restaurant sales made a career change and took an assignment with a paper goods supplier because the cups, plates and plastics ware were used by restaurants and fast food establishments. Because the client has knowledge of what restaurants used, representing a paper goods supplier was a natural fit. Another client spent years in college but could not find an immediate job. They took out an ad offering their research and writing skills to other college students and busy working adults pursuing a degree but too busy to write papers on their own. The writing business immediately took off.

Job candidates can also leverage experience and hobbies into a viable career track. If you demonstrate prior sales experience and love to play golf, a natural career option would be to seek to represent sporting goods companies offering golf equipment. Virtually any avocation can be leveraged into a job opportunity with a little research and creative thinking.

A teacher from a small town in Alabama once went to the state legislature with a plan to open a community college and walked away with a two million dollar grant as a down payment to begin construction in addition to assuming the position of president of the institution. His former tenure as a high school history teacher did not hinder him from assuming greater responsibility in an academic role. The fact he was able to conceive and present benefits for a community college in his hometown was sufficient incentive to persuade the legislature to cooperate.

BE BACKS

A "be back" is a customer who says they need time to think when they have little to no intention of coming back. In an employment context, companies convince candidates they need more time before making an offer which translates into the needing more time to interview other candidates. By generating a long list of potential candidates, the bean counters can select candidates they like who are willing to work for the least compensation. What happens to the others? They are eventually sent one of those tidy form letters, "You are a great candidate but there is no room at the inn." If you buy into a "be back" excuse from a company, you might end up defaulting on your car and house payments when you would have been better served by continued to seek another position. For those of you have been duped by the promises of others, realize the statement, "Give us more time," translates into "Keep looking." And if you are going to error, on what side do you need a cushion?

Delay comments include references to you "being the best candidate," "you are my pick," etc. Consider the traction you will get when you treat delays as rejections and continue to seek offers. If the company does get back to you, there is absolutely nothing lost. If another company gets back to you with an offer, you can use their offer to sweeten a compensation package by competing one company against another. Turn a seller's market into a buyer's market by getting as many job offers as you can. Frequently, companies pay more for what they feel they cannot easily obtain. If your services are wanted by another company, your goes up.

Beware of companies who ask you to fly on your dime for interviews in other parts of the country. They have nothing to lose and you are out travel and accommodation expenses on the promise they will get back to you with an offer. Generally such companies have numerous job candidates applying for the same position. Excuses are rampant but the bottom line is they expect you to pay for the privilege of their time and any promises they make prior to an interview are merely to lure you into spending your money for a little of their time. Such opportunities are exploitive to say the least. If a company is honestly interested in bringing you aboard, they will happily pay your travel expenses in exchange for your time. If the company is unwilling to pay your travel and lodging expenses it might suggest they are experiencing financial difficulty or are not people oriented.

THE FATIGUE METHOD

Cowboys and gauchos of old prided themselves in breaking horses using the fatigue method; they wore horses down until the horses stopped bucking. As an unfortunate side effect many horses had their spirit broken making them unfit for challenging work. American Indians were smarter; they led horses into water and then climbed atop their back. A horse cannot buck in water and learned to accept the rider without losing motivation. Private employment agencies typically fail to place over 90% of the clients who approach and frequently resort to the fatigue method to wear clients down. By throwing a large number of candidates at companies in hopes one will come away with the job, the agency makes money while the job candidates who do not receive offers are exploited. Like a spit ball, throw anything at employers hoping something will stick.

Employment agencies realize if they send job candidates on enough interviews they will eventually settle for almost anything due to their exhausted, demoralized state. Using this approach can virtually push job candidates into positions they might resent later. If you hastily accept a job that does not represent a correct fit, there are penalties for leaving the job early. You might end up having to pay the agency an early termination fee.

The more interviews you go on without positive feedback, the more you become a candidate for "learned helplessness." Should you find yourself being sent out on interviews not remotely close to your background, experience, or interest, you might consider you are being used as filler to satisfy the needs of the agency. Many companies require at agencies provide at least three job candidates for interviews. No one likes to be manipulated like a hamster in a wheel.

Possible scams to be wary of include employment agencies selling you an expensive resume and overstating the benefits of placing your resume on their webpage that rarely gets visited. Frequently employment agencies boast a high percentage of job placements but refuse to disclose them because of specious confidentiality rules designed to cover up a low percentage of placements. Beware of expensive career programs and coaching classes designed to add to the agency's bottom line more than help you find a rewarding work position.

SEARCH FIRMS

Theoretically, search firms are experts at identifying the core requirements and qualifications for a given position. Their outreach strategies search for pools of candidates they hope will match positions they have uncovered. The positions they have uncovered can be discovered by almost anyone willing to do a little research, read trade journals, utilize online networking, or place a few strategic phone calls. When looking at published promotion announcements, understand the position the employee once held might now be available. If a company expects to open a new division, work opportunities will surely accompany such a decision. Anticipating change yields career opportunities for the observant job candidate.

Search firms survive by virtue of the Chinese checker principle, placing you with a competitive company and then filling your vacancy with another client they have located so two commissions apply. Because working clients are perceived as more valuable than unemployed candidates, search firms are primarily interested in candidates who are still employed. Excitement and appetite is aroused when companies believe they must steal you from another company. This is why they are generically referred to as head hunters. Head hunters want live heads, not those already considered shrunken from unemployment. Ironically, it is widely known in the employment world search firm representatives typically work for agencies only long enough to find a better position themselves. So if you are considering using the services of a search firm, you might think in terms of working for one to find the position you want. It seems to work for others as the high turnover in the field suggests.

THE GOLDILOCKS GAME

Goldilocks was a young girl who combined her analytical decision making with her discriminating taste buds to arrive at a comparative food selection. She sampled three bowls of porridge; one too hot, one too cold, and one was just right when compared to the other two. Search firms and employment agencies use this strategy when they parade three clients in front of a potential employer. One client is overqualified. One client is barely qualified. One client appears just right when compared with the other two. If you find yourself being displayed in front of potential employers and realize the fit is not right, consider you are being manipulated to the advantage of someone else. This same approach has been used in real estate. If a customer wants a house that is beyond their income, the savvy real estate agent shows them a house beyond what they could ever afford; another dilapidated house far below what they would ever live in; and finally a third house now appearing to represent a reasonable alternative when compared with the other two homes. In psychology giving test subjects a lemon drop first, and a piece of sweet chocolate second, makes the chocolate taste even sweeter indicating how taste and perceptions can be manipulated by sequence.

A production engineer with an automotive background went to a local search firm and was informed Personnel Managers routinely came into the search firm's central office to interview candidates. The employment counselor reviewed his qualifications and saw he possess some exposure to electrical systems. The employment counselor arranged for an interview the following Monday with an electronics assembly firm. The candidate found two other candidates in the waiting room applying for the same job. The interviewer was running late so there was ample time to talk with the other two candidates about their background. One of the candidates was still working for an electrical assembly company and confided the headhunter insisted he attend the interview. The second was fresh out of school with an advanced degree in electrical engineering. It did not take the production engineer long to realize he was being used as filler for the interview. After a disappointing interview, the job candidate confronted the employment counselor regarding the poor fit. The employment counselor took the attitude he was merely trying to help the candidate get a job. Truthfully, the candidate was being used like a lemon drop to sweeten the prospects of the other two job candidates. In actuality, the candidate was there to ensure the employment counselor received a commission. You have a personal obligation to look out for your own self-interest when dealing with employment counselors. Do not accept false promises. Ask questions and insist the fit is appropriate to your experience and future career objectives before agreeing to interview for potential positions.

JOB FAIRS

Job Fairs and Career Fairs are becoming a popular side show where hopeful job candidates stand in long lines to hand their application to employment representatives who sit behind tables with smiles painted on their faces. Employment representatives are trained to give your ego a massage while hiding their true feelings i.e., you stand about as good a chance of getting a job as a snowball surviving in the desert. Companies who participate in trade shows have ingeniously found an inexpensive way to amass piles of scrap paper. Besides, it makes personnel managers look like they are doing their job. At best, job fairs are a long shot and typically result in less than 1% of the candidates getting offers, depending on the mix, intent of the fair, and the position the candidate is willing to take. A million sperm cells swimming frantically towards one egg comes to mind. When you think of it, Job Fairs are ingenious marketing strategies used by hospitality experts who have found a way to sell their facility space under the guise of helping people find jobs. In actuality, they are selling booth space to companies and receiving a percentage of profits from $5.00 hotdogs and $2.00 cups of coffee.

On the positive side, Job Fairs and Career Fairs are an opportunity to meet and learn about employers in your area. You will certainly glean information from other job candidates attending the fair. Job Fairs can provide leads and can be combined with speakers who might pass along valuable information beneficial to your job search. On the negative side, companies represented at Job Fairs are not generally the highest quality and frequently include resume companies, employment agencies and temporary employment firms looking to add to their arsenal of potential clients. Standing in line with other job candidates can diminish self-esteem and create an unsavory impression of hopelessness. Rather than confront the possibility of standing out in a crowd of 100 job candidates, why not stack the odds in your favor by submitting resumes directly to quality companies in your area with suggestions that entice interviews. When you consider most candidates would never offer suggestions in their resumes and cover letters, using the strategy will certainly cause you to stand out from the average job candidate and begins subsequent interviews with a strong first impression. Consider the impression a cover letter generates when it promises to increase sales, streamline production or reduce operating costs. Why wait for an interview to discuss suggestions. The resume and cover letter are the keys to open the door to lucrative job opportunities. Stand out from the average job candidate by cultivating a willingness to serve along with helpful suggestions. It worked for Obvious Adams so why would it not work for you?

THE HIDDEN JOB MARKET

It has been suggested the best way to hide something is to make it conspicuously obvious. This adage is particularly applicable to "hidden job markets." The hidden job market is not actually hidden. Hidden implies uncovering employment opportunities not being advertised. Statistics suggest over eighty percent of job opportunities are not advertised. Frequently companies rely on current employee networks and local job pools to avoid the flood of resume that ensue once a job opening is advertised. Career experts suggest job candidates spend no more than 20% of their time answering ads. Rather, it is suggested better results are derived through networking and direct employer contact. The strategy is to be considered for an opportunity before a job is listed. Once a job is listed, competition is inevitable.

Decision makers prefer taking the path of least resistance. Rather than sift through hundreds of applications and setting up tedious interviews, the path of least resistance favors job applicants who show initiative by contacting a company directly and offering to help the organization meet its goals. In addition to the path of least resistance there is the issue of risk avoidance. Hiring managers prefer people they know or who come highly recommended. Direct contact is an excellent way for hiring managers to get to know you without the distraction of other applicants. Job candidates can also search through blogs and forums to find a network contact who might know the hiring manager. Many network members are happy to help because they realize they can rely on your help in return.

The library holds a rich bounty of statistical information about companies job candidates can contact through direct mail, email or direct contact. Samplings of references are listed in the back of this handbook. A few hours of effective research in the library saves a great deal of shoe leather. And like the mail order companies who do not purchase products until after they measure the consumer response, candidates need not invest wasted effort learning about a specific position until they get a response for an interview.

DIRECT MAIL STATISTICS

In general, direct marketing companies operate on a 3% return factor, contingent upon the mailing list, the product, seasonal fluctuations, and the quality of the marketing presentation. This low percentage figure translates into 3 responses for each 100 resumes mailed. Not an impressive amount. Job candidates can achieve well over a 90% response when they gear their resume to a particular company's needs and target the document to the key decision maker. Documents possessing "hooks" make suggestions promising benefits. A summary of qualifications inserted into a resume suggests both what a job candidate has done and what they can do. For example, listing you can open new territories, launch new brands and service existing accounts does not mean you have done it. It means you are capable of doing it. If the company is looking for a marketing representative, your qualifications conveniently complement the needs of the position, even though your direct experience does not.

A better strategy for obtaining interviews would be to make suggestions for product enhancement, advertising, marketing or territory expansion. What decision maker would turn down an opportunity to hear ideas about how to improve the company? A client sent a letter to a fast food restaurant suggesting a modest investment would significantly increase service and sales by as much as 35% or more. During the interview with the owner the client presented an illustration showing how the addition of a drive through land and window. Along with the illustration the client provided estimates from two contractors showing the affordability of the modification. Without hesitation the client was hired to oversee the project. Once the drive through service lane proved successful, the client was made responsible for making similar modifications to other restaurants in the chain. Consider how the success story began with a simple letter to a fast food restaurant.

Sending a resume and cover letter to the president and having it passed down to a key decision maker is better than sending it to a personnel department where it gets filed with hundreds of other resumes. A personnel department is geared to finding someone to fill an existing need. The president of a company thinks in broader terms whereby opportunities can be created to accommodate change. The difference in the expectations of a personnel department and the president can vary dramatically in this sense. Start at the top when approaching companies with suggestions.

EFFECTIVE RESUMES SUGGEST CAPABILITIES

Promising suggestions and solutions gets more attention than background and experience. "Can open new territories, launch new brands and service existing accounts," are potentials. Founded upon the operative word "can," if the company is looking for a marketing representative, such qualifications conveniently complement the needs of the position, even though direct experience may not. The logic is: you aren't shooting hot air if you can do it. A student fresh out of college may have little to market but his potential, since hands-on experience in classroom settings is limited. Therefore, such a candidate would highlight specific projects if applicable, or classes taken and areas of occupational interest compatible with the needs and future objectives of the company. Tell companies what you can do for them and dramatically increase your requests for interviews. Allowing them to draw their own conclusions based on your lack of experience, limited experience or incompatible experience is playing unnecessary roulette.

Management and marketing skills are applicable to virtually any product or service. Approaching companies with a list of marketing activities you can implement will fetch interviews, even when experience is lacking. Consider the following summary of qualifications: Communications training in interpersonal psychology can convert product presentations into account revenue. Award recognition at the World Robotics Symposium has led to the development of innovative products with consumer demand. Hands-on laboratory experience in micro-particle physics can readily be applied to superconductivity research and research development. Recent academic training in management promises improved performance and productivity in virtually any manufacturing environment.

If answering an ad, it is appropriate to put the title used in the advertisement as the objective. If sending resumes directly to companies when no advertised opening exists, a more generalized objective assures maximum consideration for any available opportunities. Instead of listing an objective for a Sales Manager, you could list Sales Professional. The company may have a sales position available with a management position opening in the near future. Refrain from stating an expected level of compensation and do not include prior salary history. Companies asking for salary history are looking for job candidates who will take low compensation. Why else would they ask? Compensation is something to be negotiated after an offer is proffered.

INFORMATION ABOUT COMPANIES

There are several books online which contain a wealth of knowledge about potential companies who will make an offer if approached with benefits. Contacts Influential is a group on LinkedIn designed to bring together business oriented networkers to share ideas, opportunities and contracts. Each Chamber of Commerce publishes its own Industrial Guide of local businesses along with the names of key decision makers along with the nature of the product or service, annual sales, and number of employees. Using this resource in place of the want ads minimizes competition and results in local offers, not those requiring extended driving commitments. A few well-spent hours performing research maximizes productive interviews.

Understanding a company's product or service allows you to fine tune your qualifications as incentives. If the company is involved in manufacturing, use manufacturing incentives associated with fabrication, assembly, shipping and receiving. Annual sales can suggest salary potential. If a company displays sales less than $1,000,000, your salary requirement for $100,000 will likely be a stretch. If the majority of your experience has been with a large company with highly specific job duties, you may be unwilling or unable to accommodate the diverse responsibilities of a smaller company. Therefore, the focus of your job search would be with larger companies with defined job descriptions and responsibilities. If your prior experience lends itself to small companies, you would do well to investigate opportunities where your diverse ability to wear several hats will be positively received.

Types of information include basic contact, sales and employee size, credit reports, company outlooks, financial data, export and import information and any pending lawsuits. A few search resources involve Dialog, DataStar, Lexis-Nexis and Dow Jones. Information about companies can be further broken down by region, including United States TICKERDIR, Asia Pacific Company directories ASIACO and Canadian company directories CANADACO. Public records databases include CBD-Infotek, Information America, Lexis-Nexis and KnowX. Useful private company information can be found through Regional Business Dateline, Newspaper files, Case Law and Patent and Trademark files.

INVESTIGATING CAREER ALTERNATIVES

Old systems have the advantage of being established and understood. For new systems to prevail, new strategies for change must be developed.

MAKING A CAREER CHANGE IS EASY

Anyone can make a career change with a little improvisation. The main ingredient is convincing employers existing abilities can readily be applied to new challenges with positive results. Research a company's product or service prior to the interview. Read trade journals, articles and newspaper reports about the company. Ask friends what they know about the firm or a competitive organization. Translate prior work experience and capabilities into specific industrial buzz words. Concentrate on one industry at a time to maximize research efforts. "Scheduling" in a retail setting is typically called "manpower planning" in manufacturing environment and referred to as "staffing" in a hospital facility. Jargon makes you sound like an insider instead of a raw recruit who will need training before contributions are realized.

Consider using a little poetic license by renaming prior titles held so they are congruent with recognizable positions in the new field. The difference between an industrial engineer and a manufacturing engineer is often miniscule. A Program Manager in one setting fulfills the same job description as a Program Director in another setting. One client successfully borrowed the momentum associated with engineering occupations by renaming his last position Human Engineer. They demonstrated how prior dispatching experience involved managing people and quickly secured an interview and an offer. Convince employers you not only know something about their field, show how prior experience, skills and abilities complement the needs of the organization. Communication is thereby enhanced, making it easy for employers to make offers.

There are times when job candidates fare better in making up a job title. One client decided during an economic crunch to fall back on their cartooning skills. They visited a local copy shop and noticed customers were experiencing difficulty using the copy machines. As a solution, the client went home and drew up a few instructional cartoons and presented them to the copy center along with a few business cards with the title, Cartoonist. Very soon thereafter clients needing illustrations began to call and subsequently provided a nice income.

WHICH DIRECTION AM I MOVING?

Before considering a career change, look carefully at the situation and ask: "Am I moving towards an opportunity or away from a bad experience?" A new career can enhance motivation. Running from a bad incident may result in little more than repeating the same situation with the next company because of a personal issue. Signs of escape or avoidance in job candidates are easily detected during the interview. Employers familiar with avoidance shy away. It is prudent to refrain from disparaging your last company or employer. "I am looking for greater challenges," is good reason to change companies. "My last company tried to cheat me out of a commission," is poor marketing.

Getting fired at one time could "black ball" workers from getting jobs in the same occupational area. Recent legislation restricts companies from disclosing negative information about prior employees. Being asked to leave a company generally means the fit was not right. Although it is considered poor style to discuss negative occupational experiences during interviews, unfortunate incidents can become strong selling points when strategically portrayed. Justin Dart, the founder of Dart Drug, took such an approach when he interviewed for a job with United Drug. Dart informed the Board of Directors of the mistakes he made while with Walgreens. The Board hired him because he was actually communicating he would not be making the same mistakes twice. "Are there sufficient problems in your organization to keep me out of trouble?" is an effective use of reverse psychology. Innovators make for poor maintainers. This approach allows a discussion of a prior termination from a positive perspective. It is natural to seek out new challenges.

If reverse psychology is properly managed, the interview suddenly changes. The employer starts selling his problems to the job candidate. When drafting a resume and cover letter it is prudent not to mention you were terminated from your former assignment. Save your ammunition for the interview.

CHANGE REQUIRES ADAPTABILITY

The adage, "When in Rome do as the Romans," means adapting your background to the needs of the organization you desire affiliation with. Again, resources found online help generate immediate lists of potential work possibilities. If considering a career track, the Occupational Outlook Handbook is a handy publication that categorizes occupations, preferred requirements, range of compensation, and potential future openings. Hundreds of positions are discussed ranging from accountants to woodworkers. Next investigate categories through literature on companies, friends in the field, and fact finding interviews. Employers like to share their experiences and will volunteer valuable market information to receptive ears. A sound marketing strategy promotes employer dialogue. Encouraging decision makers to share information about their company will provide valuable insights into potential job prospects.

Many jobs look good on paper but entirely different during the interview or after taking the reins. One client thought being an architect would be exciting. They soon changed their mind when they discovered much of his job was drawing basic layouts and running blueprints. All occupations like to idealize their field. The elephant boasts of size while the cheetah brags of speed. The National Teachers Association portrays instructors as mentors surrounded by motivated learners. Many teachers see themselves as glorified baby sitters who spend most of their time attempting to maintain classroom discipline instead of teaching. If you think you would like to be a teacher and possess the necessary qualifications, volunteer to substitute teach and then make your final decision. If you still want to teach you will be making an informed decision. If you believe you will be happy in a respective career track, look for internships or part-time assignments to get your feet wet and experience the true nature of the job description.

A client was looking for a means for finishing their graduate degree and landed a Civil Service position. The candidate completed the Professional Administrative Career Exam offered by the Civil Service Administration and underwent a panel interview where job candidates were required to debate a topic with other job candidates while incumbent Civil Service professionals graded remarks. Twenty were selected for specialized training. The job looked good on paper until they realized the job involved sitting behind a desk and collating thousands of regulations. Investigate opportunities prior to accepting the offer. Have the confidence to believe you can get offers. Go for companies you want to work for, not just those who appear convenient.

Another excellent publication is the Places Rated Almanac providing evaluations of Standard Statistical Metropolitan Areas for future job opportunities, wages, and price of housing, crime, and educational resources. A client sold their home, left their job as a production foreman and bought a cabin in Montana without taking time to investigate local job opportunities. The goal was to get out of California. They soon found the local economy so depressed the only alternative was to get a job at a local feed and fuel store loading hay. Moving can be exciting and occupationally rewarding, but get facts before making important career decisions and blazing new trails across the desert in search of Eden. Let mail and email do your work for you. A well-written resume can pique a company's appetite. If sufficiently impressed, the company may forego the expense and fly you in for the interview. Make the company invest something in the opportunity to ensure reciprocal interest. Many companies have recruiters who do nothing more than to travel throughout the country to interview candidates. Stimulate companies with incentives and watch how quick the phone rings.

Clients who change assignments for new challenges make significantly more money than employees loyal to one firm. A single job is no longer practical in a rapidly changing economics. Jobs are situational assignments where skills and abilities are applied to the problems of the day. Lessons learned on prior assignments can readily be leveraged into new job descriptions. Thrive on challenges and enjoy solving problems for others and watch your corporate worth soar. Too many paths have been trodden by candidates fulfilling the requirements of a low paying mundane job when they are capable of much more. Happiness is proportional to the extent abilities are utilized. "Use it or lose it," translates into career growth or decay. Knowing there are organizations looking for ambitious problem solvers means you never have to be intimidated by a depressing job description again.

GETTING STARTED

Journeys pointed in right directions reach desired destinations.

Robert Frost is well known for his poem, The Road Not Taken, depicting his choice to become a poet. In borrowing the analogy, the trodden road taken by the majority of career candidates leads to the want ads where they are asked to be molded into an existing job description. Take the initiative to create an exciting job assignment by mastering the fundamentals of career marketing outlined in this handbook. Career development is a life long journey not a static destination. Time spent learning marketing techniques is an investment in occupational fulfillment and greater compensation. Once offers are accepted interpersonal persuasion skills will ensure growth within the organizational hierarchy. Be wary of believing everything promised during the interview unless it is in writing. Unscrupulous employers will say anything to get you on board, realizing you will fear rocking the boat once you accept the position. False promises include salary reviews, potential raises, upcoming promotions, benefits and training. It is paramount expectations are clarified for both parties when an offer is extended. Many candidates become disillusioned when raises are not forthcoming in a timely manner. Why set yourself up for disappointment. Talk to existing employees about raises and promotions prior to accepting an offer. Frequently they will give you a more realistic picture of what will occur.

With persistence and correct marketing, increased compensation and job satisfaction is provided in return for your labor. Wise farmers identify future needs so they will not plant unprofitable crops. In a career context, this means you will need to investigate new career opportunities to guarantee viability in the future market. Many experts correctly anticipated the advent and growth of the computer revolution. What they didn't anticipate was the low pay associated with the majority of data entry computer positions. Where programming jobs are on the rise, much of the available software has become so sophisticated; off-the-shelf versions typically satisfy many company needs. More computer users are involved in keeping abreast with new programs and updates over writing custom programs. Debugging computers is now commonplace. It doesn't take an expert to follow a menu.

Just as wise farmers diversify crops to anticipate fluctuating weather and market conditions; it is wise to diversify resume mailings and job search strategies. Like seasonal fluctuations affect crop yield, businesses also change throughout the year. Many companies implement a hiring freeze towards the end of the year until the accountants inform them how well they did. Wine and spirit companies close their year out in September so their accounting year begins on the last quarter, their strongest months. There are many companies hiring during Christmas. Plant lots of seeds so your excitement builds with each trip to the mailbox. Attempting to market your skills to the wrong company is like volunteering to be miscast. There are literally thousands upon thousands of companies and decision makers looking for quality job candidates. The problem is selection and notification. A positive attitude is the result of having something good to look forward to. This is the foundation upon which goal setting is based.

FINDING THE RIGHT WORK ENVIRONMENT

Many inventions were overlooked because they failed to complement the needs of their time. The steam engine was considered a toy long before it was seriously applied to work. The wheel became the major means of transportation in Europe while used for making pottery in America during the same period. Both continents had different needs. You can possess outstanding skills and receive miniscule compensation when attempting to launch your career in an organizational setting unable to recognize and take advantage of your specialty. Understanding your passion and translating it into a valued contribution in a compatible organizational setting is crucial to job fulfillment and compensation.

Work environments are similar to different countries; they each have their respective culture. Wise career coaches teach career success is the result of finding the correct culture so your contributions fill the perceived needs of the organization. Interview with confidence and during the interview ask decision makers how they see your specialized skills and abilities contributing to the forward momentum of the firm. Forget fitting into a predestined spot. Negotiate your own job description by offering more benefits than employees currently on board.

Things to consider in assessing a work environment are the demeanor of the staff. Do employees dress formal or informal? Is there an emphasis on structure or is the work environment somewhat unstructured? Do staff members appear happy or subdued? Are they competitive or cooperative? Is there an emphasis on creativity or routine? Is there a sense of purpose among the staff or does the culture appear bored and tedious? Does the organization employ cubicles or does everyone work in an open area? Will the position involve commuting or is the assignment close to home? It is not just about finding a job; it is about finding a place where your passions can be engaged.

MEA CULPA

Sorry...

Interviews are predominately psychological. Having a good resume opens the door. The critical element in achieving a successful offer involves the ability to interpersonally project skills, abilities and solutions applicable to the needs of the organization. Unemployed candidates tend to depreciate their experience and qualifications regardless of prior accomplishments. Answering questions in a downcast, hangdog fashion significantly minimizes market appeal. No one likes to buy wilted lettuce. This is called the Mea Culpa Syndrome, "I have sinned - please hire me anyway." Scraping and groveling fetches peanuts for compensation because employers are convinced you must prove your worth all over again.

When we want to work and cannot find work, frustration insinuates itself into every crevice of our lives. The fact a cessation in work does not mean the bills stop coming can lead to a demoralized state of mind. Interpersonal psychology shows people wipe their feet on you when you lie down like a doormat. Approaching a company with optimistic ideas and benefits is profoundly critical because advantages are future-oriented. Old style stereotypes perpetuate the belief a cut in pay is necessitated when changing jobs. This faulty perception is predicated on negatives associated with leaving a company. Companies are willing to be convinced your hard earned experience can be had for less. This thought process is indicative of inexperienced retailers who tend to lower the price on merchandise when sales are slow. Wise retailers create interesting displays to increase product turnover. Why volunteer to be underpaid and underutilized. Dress up your qualifications with incentives for the next firm.

A FEW FACTS AND MYTHS ABOUT RESUMES

Truth is the most direct route to prosperity.

THE MASOCHISTIC APPROACH TO CAREER SUCCESS

The Law of Instrument states when you rear a child with a hammer they grow up to see the world as a nail. Picture the following scenario: We get up in the morning and go out and get the newspaper in order to spend the next hour pouring over the want ads with a cup of coffee affixed to our left hand, and a red marker poised in our right. If we really want to get organized we have scissors and tape within reach so we can post on a blank sheet of paper possible opportunities we may wish to respond to with a resume. In between trips to the bathroom to rid ourselves of caffeine we curse the idiots who write the ad copy. Somewhere between A and Z and our seventh cup of coffee we experience waves of frustration quickly leading to doubt. The more ads we clip the more frustrated and doubtful we become. Sound familiar? This is not a recipe for career success.

PRIORITIZE YOUR JOB HUNTING

An unfocused job search translates into taking what you can get. This often means driving miles to a position and receiving less money to pay for gas. It does not take long before the extended drive, particularly in heavy traffic, takes its toll on motivation. Fatigue at work means you might be overlooked for future job promotions. Why not eliminate such a result by seeking jobs in your general area first. Effective job hunting begins with prioritization. If unfamiliar with the various communities in your area, secure a local map for use when investigating references in the library or try Google Maps when searching online. In the modern world, a street view allows job candidates to observe the appearance of work facilities without ever leaving the computer. Although some publications cross companies by location, others use a SIC (Standard Industrial Code) and list firms in alphabetical order. You can save wasted time by checking your map for unfamiliar locations. Start with those located in a five mile radius. Presidents and managers tend to move often in today's world of work so get the most recently published resource to ensure your resume stands the best chance of getting to the current decision maker.

Create a pre-dated work board upon which to list things to do using the calendar on your smart phone or computer. If you are a hands-on type, you can create a work board by cutting squares from an inexpensive wall calendar and pasting the days, sequentially, on the pages of a legal tablet. Spacing the squares so as to minimize overlap on successive pages eliminates an annoying hump in the tablet. The electronic or manual work board allows you to schedule upcoming activities while keeping a handy record of things done. Copy anything not accomplished from one day to the next by order of importance. The work board allows you to keep track of important, upcoming appointments and to look back at dates when resumes were mailed and telephone calls placed. Use it as a diary for making critical notes. It not only serves as an operations tool it is self-reinforcing when you see the progress made in a short amount of time. Work board Example:

Sent Resumes June 1, 2012:
J.P. Williams and Co. 2332 West Euclid, Los Angeles.
Sent to the Bill Johnson, President.
IBM, Inc., 1414 Roanoke Rd. Los Angeles, CA
Reynolds Aluminum, 679 Winchester Drive, Corona.
Adas Packaging, 229 Broad Street, San Bernardino.

Follow-up Calls June 1, 2012:
Amex Petroleum (Jack Peters) RE: Resume sent 5-19-2012.
Company stated they might be opening a new territory this month.
Standard Oil (Alex Smith) RE: Resume sent 5-23-2012.
Manager will be back from vacation and will review my resume.

Interviews June 1, 2012:
11:00 Jackson Mfg. 445 Eugene Avenue, Colton.
Contact person is Bill Jackson.
1:00 Saunders Inf. Systems, 45 Block St. Colton.
Meeting with Leslie Ferguson, Training Director.
2:45 AAA Plastics, 224 Amethyst, Rancho Cucamonga.
Trade journal states they are expanding to Northern California.

Keep record of all resumes and letters sent alphabetically by company name on a rolodex next to the phone for handy reference. When a telephone call comes from an employer, find out what company they represent then stall by telling the employer you need to get to another phone for privacy. Scan your rolodex for the company name and your notes i.e., whether you responded to an advertisement and what position you were after. The rolodex or spreadsheet can substitute for your work board.

Company Name: ABE Plastics Address: Corona, CA
Phone No: (714)694-2337 Contact: Jones/President
Ad Class: Production Foreman Disposition: Resume 4/91
Company Name: Johnson Paste Address: 1120 South Street.
Phone No: (714)770-0000 Contact: Jack Hire/Controller
Ad Class: Financial Planner Disposition: Resume 8/91

ONE OUT OF MANY

Resumes have become a prerequisite for landing most jobs in our time. In fact, over 98% of white collar positions now require a resume as a means of prescreening potential candidates. Many blue collar job openings require applications in addition to resumes because busy decision makers do not want unproductive interviews. Resumes tell more about the style of a job candidate than an application. Resume statistics suggest over fifty percent of resumes contain falsifications. Over seventy percent of college students stated they would lie on a resume to get the job they want. Learning how to present ideas is a better strategy than resume deception that can backfire at a later date.

THE NEEDLE IN THE HAYSTACK

Research points out some companies receive as many as a quarter of a million resumes a year. This number translates into a significant amount of reading. Who sifts through the stack? Generally a low paid personnel drone. What approach do drones take? Typically the process of elimination! Other numbers point to the fact candidates receive an invitation to interview for every 250 resumes read. Small wonder job seeking begins to look like an upstream swim. Many clients make the mistake of going only for the Fortune 500 companies; the ones receive the most resumes. Small companies can afford excellent opportunities as well as well as much less competition. As the adage suggests, "It is sometimes better to be a big frog in a little pond, than a little frog in a big pond."

Job statistics state over fifty percent of full-time hires were from internal transfers and promotions which means job candidates must ensure their presentation is of sufficient magnitude to convince companies to consider hiring outside of the establishment. Almost twenty five percent of external hires are attributable to referrals, placing tremendous emphasis on networking. Job boards accounted and career sites now account for approximately thirty-five percent of new hires. Third party recruiters accounted for a mere 2.3 percent of external hires. The remaining 23 percent were attributable to job candidates walking through the door and seeking jobs. Encounter less competition for an opening by creating opportunities by approaching companies directly.

INTEREST NOT BIAS

Candidates can minimize wasted effort by insuring their resume creates interest, not bias. Far too many resumes are loaded with detrimental information. The effective resume is the one is most difficult to invalidate. This does not suggest a resume so nebulous it fails to communicate potential benefits to an employer. What it means is excluding items like former salary, age, weight, hobbies and religious preference.

If you possess a degree in real estate and are not applying for a position in the field, put down you have a degree without specifying in what area. Get the interview and then explain why you went to school in one field and wish to work in another. A common mistake is for women to include they are active in the PTA, thereby impressing employers with their parental responsibility. Unfortunately, what they convey is a potential conflict between child care and work. Emphasizing former union affiliation when going for a management position can raise eyebrows unless the job candidate suggests they can use their former union experience to satisfy negotiation objectives.

A pilot insisted on including weekend motorcycle racing as a hobby on their resume. As predicted, they received no offers because conservative airlines shy away from high risk profiles. List achievements which can be marketed as solutions to companies and you will suddenly see a rise in employer interest. Start qualifications with such words as Accelerated, Coordinated, Developed, Established, Fostered, Generated, Implemented, Justified, Leveraged, Managed, Organized, Optimized, Procured, Reduced, Saved, and Tested and watch how potential employers take the hook.

For example, "Accelerated production rates by as much as 20% in as little as three months through the implementation of methods improvements." As another example, "Developed a capital justification for additional equipment for a dramatic reduction in scrap; saved the company over $325,000 during the first six months."

WE DO JUDGE A BOOK BY ITS COVER

When it comes to resumes we do judge a book by its cover. Resumes placed inside expensive covers create a vastly different impression than single sheet documents on fifteen pound paper from a copy machine. Candidates often overlook the power of image. Image is the sum total of details. Since the resume is the first image many employers see, it is critical the resume convey interest and power. There is a relationship between image and the level of compensation sought. Overlooking details leads to reduced compensation. The status score you receive is directly related to your subsequent salary and respect in the organization.

Some resumes are so poorly written and ill-conceived it is miraculous job candidates get interviews at all. It is both what you say but how you say it. Attention to details and vocabulary sets the tone and many professional resume consultants are recommending clients include action words to create interest. Used judiciously, such terms as maximized, stimulated, optimized and initiated can transform a mundane document into a dynamic marketing proposal. Too many adjectives inflate the document with hot air and raises suspicions.

THE ONE PAGE MYTH

A favorite old school myth mandates putting all your experience and abilities on one page because "busy decision makers will read no more." Executives buy and read more books than most professionals. They will continue to read as long as a document is pertinent and interesting. One-page frequently does not permit sufficient disclosure to allow employers to separate the problem solver from the sedentary desk potato. One-page documents are sufficient for entry level positions and candidates earning less than $30,000 a year. Higher paying positions need one full page to portray qualifications and education alone. Subsequent pages present experience as supporting documentation for the qualifications. If resumes are too brief, employers will call someone else. Three pages is often appropriate; one page for a summary and education; another page for experience; and a third page for the persuasive cover letter.

CHRONOLOGICAL FORMATS

Resumes differ from applications because they are designed as strategic marketing devices. Applications require a chronological list of past positions. Resumes can list prior positions in any sequence you want as long as the sequence makes sense, has focus, and emphasizes benefits. If you changed fields several times, including dates in a chronological format encourages unfavorable employer bias. Research shows resumes can be effective without dates if they strategically communicate benefits to pique the employer's self-interest. Response is the acid test. If you are not getting response, consider changing your resume. This is what direct mail advertising campaigns frequently do. An alternative to listing dates on your resume is to list number of years. When describing your present position you can merely type "Present," rather than telling how little time you have worked for a company. Eliminate dates of graduation from schools which make it easy for employers to calculate your age. Documents hardest to invalidate or attribute bias fetch the most response.

POWER WORDS

Power words help sell the sizzle. Consider judiciously incorporating the following words into your presentation.

Abated, abolished, abridged, absolved, accelerated, accomplished, achieved, accentuated, accommodated, accumulated, acquired, achieved, adopted, adjusted, aided, addressed, administered, advised, allocated, analyzed, anticipated, attained, applied, appraised, arranged, assigned, assured, averted, audited and awarded.

Budgeted, bolstered, boosted, broadened, built and balanced.

Calculated, caused, changed, championed, combined, compiled, condensed, consummated, converted, corrected, cleared, coded, commanded, complimented, completed, computed, conceived, conducted, consolidated, contracted, controlled, coordinated and created.

Debugged, decoded, delegated, deployed, determined, diagnosed, differentiated, defined, demonstrated, distributed, doubled, designed, developed, devised, directed and documented.

Earned, elevated, enabled, engineered, enhanced, ensured, equipped, eliminated, enlarged, enlisted, entered, established, estimated, evaluated, examined, executed, expanded, expedited, explored and extended.

Fabricated, facilitated, fashioned, finalized, fixed, formulated, financed, forecasted, founded, fulfilled, funded and founded.

Gained, generated, gauged, grouped, guaranteed, granted, guided and gathered.

Halted, handled, halved, heightened, hosted, honed, and helped.
Identified, implemented, imported, instituted, improved, incorporated, increased, initiated, innovated, installed, instructed, introduced, invented, investigated, isolated and issued.

Joined, justified and judged.

Kept.

Launched, learned, leveraged, linked, loaded, listed, led and logged.

Maintained, managed, manufactured, merged, minimized, measured, mediated, met, modified, monitored, multiplied, moved and motivated.

Navigated, netted, normalized, notified and negotiated.

Opened, obtained, offset, orchestrated, ordered, originated, outperformed, overcame, overhauled, operated, oversaw and organized.

Participated, penetrated, persuaded, prescribed, prevented, perceived, performed, persuaded, planned, prepared, presented, processed, procured, protected, programmed, prohibited, projected, proposed, provided, published, purchased, and pursued.

Questioned, quadrupled, quantified and quoted.

Ranked, rated, realized, received, recommended, reconciled, recorded, recruited, redesigned, reduced, regulated, rehabilitated, reorganized, repaired, replaced, represented, researched, resolved, restored, revamped, and revised.

Saved, scheduled, selected, served, serviced, sequenced, shortened, simplified, set up, shaped, shared, simplified, solved, started, streamlined, stimulated, strengthened, structured, substituted, supervised, and systematized.

Tackled, targeted, taught, terminated, transmitted, traced, tracked, traded, trained, transferred, transformed, trimmed, and tripled.

Unified, uncovered, undertook, utilized and updated.

Verified, validated, and volunteered.

Widened, weighed, worked, won and wrote.

Avoid excessive use of professional jargon which potentially alienates the reader. Since you never know who will be reading the resume, it is safer to make it comprehensible. If you know your subject matter you should be able to state it eloquently. The higher executives ascend the corporate ladder, the simpler and more direct the dialogue. Jargon is defined as a vocabulary peculiar to a particular profession. Elected officials are gifted with jargon. Notice the difference in stating you increased sales versus suggesting you augmented client transactions. Avoid dramatic disclosures like, "Hands-on engineer seeks increased responsibility in a botanical environment for purposes of providing botanical horticulture assistance to a diverse clientele. Reader Translation: The man mows lawns and trims hedges.

PERCENTAGES BETTER

Percentages are frequently more significant than stating numbers because percentages suggest ratios. Saving a company $100,000 in one company may seem a mere pittance in a larger organization. Therefore, paring 22% off of a budget might suggest a more dramatic achievement because the reader automatically compares the percentage to their respective fiscal situation. Stating you increased sales by 40% is far more dramatic than stating you took one account and converted it into two. Ranges, like percentages, are also dramatic. Supervise from 40 to 100 employees is a stronger statement than a staff of approximately 40. This is particularly applicable to seasonal fluctuations. Positive psychology suggests listing the highest number or a range from the average to the highest to gain the greater acceptance.

While on the subject of percentages, it is helpful to begin thinking in terms of percentages when discussing marketing share during interviews. A handy way of determining market share of a given company is to divide the total amount of goods provided by companies selling similar widgets by the total number of goods sold by the company you are interviewing with and multiply this result by 100 to find the market share expressed as a percentage. For example, if five companies sell $500 million in product; divide $100 million by $500 million to get .20 times 100 for 20 percent. Your prospective company has twenty percent of the market. This factor is useful if you are suggesting ways to increase sales for greater market share.

AVOID RESTRICTIVE OBJECTIVES

Restrictive resume objectives are exclusive rather than inclusive. The function of a resume objective is to focus the reader on the position you are seeking. The more general the resume objective the more general the interviews with exception of excessively general resumes that might not pique interest. If you are convinced you will accept a position within limited parameters, state your preference. If you are open to opportunity, generalize the objective to appeal to a wider market. Refrain from making the objective overly generic which appears unfocused or desperate for anything. The most significant skills and abilities are to be listed first. Since many exciting job opportunities are not advertised, generalizing your objective allows decision makers latitude in what positions they might consider the correct fit for your background and skill set. For example, Tool Sales Representative may not be an effective as sales specialist when it comes to market appeal. Sales is generically applicable to a wide range of opportunities tool sales is somewhat restrictive.

HIGHLITE THE GOODIES

Highlight applicable Skills, abilities and duties and write notes on your resume for a more personal touch. Most candidates have been reared to be perfectionistic when it comes to resumes making their resume merely one of the many. The strategic use of bold print, italic print and underline functions can add emphasis to your resume. Centering text is acceptable but text aligned left is easier to read. Justified text looks nice but non-justified text, like aligned left text, is easier to read. Single spacing is allowed and margins should be one inch on all sides. Space text to eliminate orphans and widows. Use twelve or fourteen font size. Arial font is easy to read and offends no one. If you do not have a word processing program, or do not like Word, perform an internet search for www.Openofficeorg, and download a free word processing program rated five stars by CNET. The same site also provides free program for spread sheets. The free programs are applicable for both Windows and Mac.

RESUME DON'TS

Resumes are marketing instruments with hooks to impress decision makers to grant interviews. For maximum acceptance, refrain from strategies potentially causing negative impacts.

Do not send references with your resume. References deserve anonymity until a serious offer is tendered. Giving employers too much information reduces their reason for contacting you. Even if interviews are allowed for no other reason than to ask questions about your resume, they still allow you opportunity for dialogue with the employer. When employers associate paper with your personality, your resume is most likely to remain on the top of the stack.

Do not fold resumes for insertion into standard mailing envelopes. Small envelopes are cheap and come across like junk mail. The act of unfolding your document reduces its market impact. A technique worth considering is to include a self-addressed stamped envelope with your resume. The employer will feel compelled to use it.

Do not mail resumes in color coordinated envelopes. Colored envelopes look like wedding invitations rather than business documents. Mail your resume in a 9x11 manila or white envelope with a typed label affixed. Manila color discourages smudge when traveling through the mail giving a better impression.

Do not sign cover letters with any other color than black. Black is the color of the business world - not green, blue, pink or gold. Be sure to sign directly over your name. Signatures are telling. Large signatures suggest inflated egos. Small signatures suggest problems with self-esteem. Awkward signatures suggest a lack of education.

Do not include marriage status, children, religious preference, weight, height age, or other potentially discriminating information. Adding such information can immediately disqualify a job candidate.

Do not copy resumes on bright colored paper. Light parch tones are appropriate, but loud or garish paper is verboten. The texture of the paper conveys a message. Cheap copy paper suggests a mass mailing campaign. Use 20 pound paper with 25% rag fiber content.

Do not send resumes to Personnel Departments or Departments of Human Resources unless no other recourse is available. Do a little investigating to reveal the decision maker. Send it to them or to the President of the company if all else fails. Resumes coming from the top down are better received than resumes passed from the bottom up. Resumes coming from the top suggest tacit approval or carry extra weight because it is understood the resume has been reviewed by a higher authority.

Data and information are different. Data represents the raw compilation of facts. Information conveys meaning by superimposing organization on collected data. A chronological resume demonstrating facts fails to communicate ideas. Professional resumes motivate employers by presenting facts in a refreshing, creative manner. On the following pages please note a few resume examples that turned into employment opportunities.

RESUME EXAMPLES

JACK M. BOSWELL
Physical address customarily goes here
Email address customarily goes here
Phone number customarily goes here

Thank you for the opportunity to present an outline of my sales and marketing qualifications. A summary of my qualifications includes augmenting regional market share through the successful management of five distributor organizations encompassing 20 sales representatives. I routinely provide strategic field troubleshooting support to identify and correct account dysfunctions, resulting in enhanced retention, repeat sales and referrals. I also attend distributor sales calls and have proven my ability to secure accounts, service existing transactions, open new territories and launch specialized products and services.

My advertising, direct mail and telecommunications expertise is backed by trade show presentations to leverage leads into viable accounts. I am capable of servicing a large number of accounts as well as multiple product categories and can expedite field repairs for enhanced customer satisfaction. I also provide for extensive distributor training while securing specialists for strategic product presentations to enhance product visibility and competitive sales awareness. Finally, my extensive electronic service experience is supported by digital electronic troubleshooting, project management experience, and field service exposure on both national and international levels.

An interview will allow me to discuss in greater detail how my background and experience, in addition to my ability to adapt quickly to new settings, can assist you in accomplishing your organizational objectives.

Sincerely,

Jack M. Boswell

JACK M. BOSWELL

Sales and Marketing professional with Management expertise seeks new challenges for augmenting regional market share.

Summary of Qualifications

o Progressive experience in management supported by extensive sales and marketing expertise to generate additional account revenue and augment regional market share.

o Have successfully managed five distributor organizations encompassing 20 sales representatives, providing strategic field support and marketing assistance for significant growth.

o Operational competence includes sales forecasting, both monthly and annually, sales itineraries, and account administration to track leads and provide factory feedback on lead follow-up.

o Comprehensive ability to secure accounts, service existing transactions, open new territories and launch specialized products and services.

o Extensive troubleshooting and problem solving skills to rapidly identify and correct account dysfunctions for enhanced retention, repeat sales and referrals.

o Demonstrated proficiency with market data analysis and demographics for improved penetration and effective client needs assessments.

o Sound advertising, direct mail and telecommunications expertise is backed by trade show presentations in order to leverage leads into viable accounts.

o Capable of servicing a large number of accounts as well as multiple product categories while interfacing with service to expedite field repairs for enhanced customer satisfaction.

o High energy personality who can interface with individuals from diverse cultural backgrounds on a national and international level for enhanced cooperation and rapport.

o Staff training and development abilities include securing specialists for strategic distributor presentations for enhance product visibility and competitive sales characteristics.

o Extensive electronics service experience is supported by digital electronics troubleshooting, project management experience, and field service exposure.

o Able to adapt quickly to new organizational settings and can convert current client account base into new sales.

Education

Numerous trainings in sales by Carl Henry, and in grinding principles with Dr. Stewart Salmon. Additional factory instruction with Jones and Shipman in London, England.

CONTROL DATA INSTITUTE, Los Angeles, CA Certificate, Computer Technology. 750 class hours -150 hands-on hours in computer technology.

Professional Experience

BAXTER MACHINES, New York, NY

Present: Over twenty years' experience with this sales and service organization offering micro-processed controlled grinding machine products to the United States and Canada. As a Regional Sales Manager, set up the West Coast distribution network to escalate sales from $ 1/2 million to approximately $ 2 million through strong commitment to existing and newly selected distributors.

Manage five distributor organizations and 20 sales representatives. Position necessitates extensive distributor training. Secure specialists for strategic seminar presentations to enhance product visibility and competitive product features over other products.

Routinely perform extensive troubleshooting and problem solving in order to rapidly identify and correct account dysfunctions for enhanced customer satisfaction, repeat sales and referrals. Apply analytical decision making proficiency to bid proposals, contract negotiations and contract administration. Attend sales calls with distributor sales representatives to provide marketing support and lend technical assistance.

Interface with service to expedite field repairs, while making factory recommendations for improved product reliability. Expedite trade show presentations to convert leads into viable accounts. Call directly on accounts to secure additional account revenue. Follow-up on factory leads both personally and with sales representatives, providing factory feedback. Position necessitates extensive travel.

* * *

Prior position with company encompassed functioning as a Field Service Engineer where I applied strong technical analytical skills to the installation, repair and instruction of basic operation and maintenance of field placed equipment, both nationally and internationally.

Lawrence Peterson

EDWARD R. LAYTON

Thank you for the opportunity to present an outline of my qualifications. I am interested in applying for your position of Senior Marketing Representativeto further U.S. and overseas military objectives.

My Program Office experience is supported by senior management expertise in both aerospace and Air Force settings and I display work affiliation with such government agencies as DoD and NASA for strategic aerospace system development. I have provided input regarding future system modifications for significant increases in performance and cost effectiveness, utilizing my troubleshooting skills to function as a liaison between customers and on-site facilities. My analytical decision making abilities allow for workable solutions to design, manufacturing and operational dysfunctions while my administrative competence includes budgeting, forecasting, and projecting.

Moreover, my procurement and manufacturing expertise includes the ability to service a large number of accounts and multiple product categories. I exhibit master scheduling and manpower planning abilities for the maximization of capital and human resources and can readily apply my well-developed oral and written communication skills for effective stand-up presentations.

An interview will allow me to discuss in greater detail how my background and experience, in addition to my ability to adapt quickly to new settings, can assist you in accomplishing your marketing objectives.

Sincerely,

Edward R. Layton

Edward R. Layton

Military Marketing specialist seeks increased responsibility in a DoD environment where technical background and marketing experience can satisfy U.S. and overseas military objectives.

Summary of Qualifications

Program office experience firmly supported by senior management expertise in both aerospace and Air Force settings.

Work affiliation with such government agencies as DoD and NASA for strategic aerospace system development.

Provide input regarding future system modifications for significant increases in performance and cost effectiveness.

Troubleshooting skills are complemented by liaison activities between customers and on-site facilities, resulting in enhanced organizational efficiency.

License

Commercial Pilot - 4000 USAF Navigation hours and over 2000 Commercial Pilot ASMEL hours

Professional Experience

T.R.W., Space and Defense. Redondo Beach, CA
Assistant Project Manager responsible for satisfying a variety of on-going program initiatives encompassing Quality Assurance, Reliability, System Safety and Configuration Management on major DoD and NASA satellite programs. Prepared numerous proposals for satellite systems and associated ground equipment while interfacing with government program office representatives relative to the overall performance of deliverable systems. Activities included proposal development in response to the RFP and the SOW. Initiated program plans, conducted

submittal presentations, and responded to government fact-finding sessions. Also substantiated estimates during contract negotiations.

Developed subcontractors for subsystem hardware and investigated problems associated with sub-contractor and in-house manufactured hardware. Resolved electro-mechanical hardware problems through corrective action plans. Monitored unit subsystem and system integration inspections along with testing and documentation for customer briefings entailing system integrity for delivery and operational use. Conducted periodic briefings and prepared reports to government program office personnel on system status toward meeting system delivery dates. Also established and maintained control of $5 Million annual budget in accordance with government contract C-SPEC requirements. Hired and supervised approximately 100 direct and indirect personnel including technical and administrative staff members.

Other company held positions included Quality Assurance Manager responsible for Quality Control of hi-rel electronic and mechanical hardware. As Staff Manager of the Group Assurance Audits Office, directed planning, conducted system audits, reported results and ensured implementation of corrective actions. Functioned as a Staff Engineer in order to prepare technical program plans and cost estimates for spacecraft proposals. Also held various field positions for preparing and launching rocket propulsion vehicles in addition to preparing service manuals, bulletins and handbooks for maintaining, servicing and repairing aircraft systems.

* * *

Prior experience includes Mobilization Augmented to the Chief of Safety, Air Force Inspection and Safety Center; Colonel, USAF, Retired; USAF Navigator, 4000 hours, bomber and transport aircraft; and General Aviation Aircraft Salesman.

PAUL K. WALTER

Thank you for the opportunity to present an outline of my qualifications. In addition to possessing seven years' experience in Respiratory Therapy Care, a summary of my qualifications includes specialized knowledge in neonatal intensive care as well as various adult and pediatric modalities. I routinely provide strategic recommendations for new equipment to enhance neonatal care and have conducted in-service trainings for physicians, nurses, new staff therapists and students on new equipment applications.

Moreover, I demonstrate the ability to function effectively in pressure situations while exhibiting team leadership to foster enhanced performance and commitment to healthcare initiatives. My well-developed oral and written communication skills result in enhanced rapport and cooperation with affiliated medical personnel. Finally, I display prior marketing experience pertinent to new account development. Furthermore, I have participated in an on-going research project for billing and physiological data recording, along with subsequent analysis for enhanced compliance with insurance requirements.

An interview will allow me to discuss in greater detail how my background and experience, in addition to my ability to adapt quickly to new settings, can assist you in accomplishing your healthcare objectives.

Sincerely,

Paul K. Walter, RCP, CRTT

Paul K. Walter, RCP, CRTT

Respiratory Therapy Care:

Seven years' experience in Respiratory Therapy Care with experience and qualifications in the following areas:

o Possess specialized knowledge in neonatal intensive care in addition to various adult and pediatric modalities.

o Routinely provide strategic recommendations for equipment and therapeutic applications resulting in improved cardiopulmonary status.
o Well-developed oral and written communication skills for enhanced rapport and cooperation with clients and affiliated medical personnel.

o Can identify potential equipment applications for enhanced neonatal care as well as provide in-service training for physicians, nurses, new staff therapists and students on new equipment applications.

o Demonstrate the ability to function effectively in pressure situations while exhibiting team leadership to foster enhanced performance and commitment to healthcare initiatives.
o Marketing experience includes the ability to open new accounts as well as service existing accounts.
Licenses and Certifications

o   NBRC CERTIFICATION - CRTT, "Registry Eligible."
o   CALIFORNIA STATE RCP LICENSE Expires: 1/31/93
o   BCLS INSTRUCTOR CERTIFICATION
o   ACLS NEONATAL RESUSCITATION CERTIFICATION.

Education:

UNIVERSITY OF CALIFORNIA, Riverside, CA Specialization: Biology Scholastic Leadership Scholarship.

MOUNT SAN ANTONIO COLLEGE, Walnut, CA Specialization:

Respiratory Therapist Program A.S. in Respiratory Therapy, Dean's Honor List. A.A. In Liberal Arts, Dean's Honor List.

Professional Experience

VALLEY MEDICAL CENTER
Neonatal Respiratory Care Practitioner
In addition to serving as a member of the Transport and Neonatal Resuscitation Team, routinely respond to all neonatal codes, C-sections and high risk deliveries. Administer aerosolized, intra-tracheal and intramuscular medications, and such mechanically ventilated airway management as endotracheal intubations. Other activities include CBG/ABG sampling and analysis, CPR, transcutaneous C02,02, and saturation monitoring. Exogenous Surfactant administration. Equipment: Sechrist Infant Ventilator, Infant Star Ventilator, Corning ABG analyzer, high flow oxygen and humidity delivery systems.
PROGRESSIVE PEDIATRICS, INCORPORATED
Respiratory Care Practitioner-Field Representative/Patient Manager
Instruct parents in the use of apnea monitors, oxygen delivery, aerosol therapy, ventilators and feeding pumps, as well as CPR training. Conduct pnuemocardiograms, polysomnograms, and oximetry studies. Provide on-going follow-up regarding patient contracts for continued patient monitoring and clinical updates. Meet with referral centers/provider groups for current updates in discharge planning. Provide in-service training to physicians and nurses on new durable medical equipment.
Equipment: Aequitron 9200, 9500, 9550, Edentech 2000W and 2000W Memory Module, Corometrics 500E Apnea Monitors, PB2800 andLifecare LP4 Ventilators, Aequitron 9100 Pneumogram Recording System and Edentrace 4 Channel Recording System, Devilbiss Pulmoaides and Corometrics Kangaroo Pumps.

MODERN THERAPY SERVICES, INCORPORATED
Respiratory Care Practitioner-Field Representative/Patient

Lawrence Peterson

Manager

Responsible for Pediatric Respiratory Home Care, including instructing parents in the use of Apnea Monitors, ventilators, pulmoaides, compressors andhome oxygen, as well as CPR procedures. Recorded and transmitted two-channel pneumograms. Provided on-going follow-up through patient contacts for continued patient monitoring and clinical updates.

Equipment: Aequitron 8200/9200 Apnea Monitors, PB-2800/ LP-4 Ventilators, PCS-4 Compressors, Two-Channel Pneumograms - Oxford Recorder, Aequitron.

BRIEN L. COOPER

Thank you for the opportunity to present an outline of my qualifications. I am a Management specialist who presently seeks increased responsibility in a challenging environment in order that my diverse background can be efficiently applied to the satisfaction of organizational objectives.

A summary of my qualifications includes seasoned management experience supported by a track record for significantly improving operational efficiency. My operational expertise includes budgeting, forecasting and auditing proficiency pertinent to virtually all operational areas, from accounting to distribution. I routinely provide troubleshooting support to rapidly diagnose and remedy operational dysfunctions while effectively interfacing with management, key decision makers and affiliated personnel to clarify and further organizational policies.

Moreover, I have served as a resource person for new account development and security system analysis, and have consistently demonstrated my ability for functioning effectively in pressure situations to meet crisis situations. I am also capable of hiring, scheduling, evaluating, training and motivating staff personnel for enhanced performance, productivity and organizational commitment. Finally, my communication skills are supported by staff meetings and newsletter article initiation to promote awareness to security initiatives.

An interview will allow me to discuss in greater detail how my background and experience, in addition to my ability to adapt quickly to new settings, can assist you in accomplishing your organizational objectives.

Sincerely,

Lawrence Peterson

Brien L. Cooper

BRIEN L. COOPER

Management specialist seeks increased responsibility in a challenging sales and service setting.

Summary of Qualifications

o Extensive experience in management supported by a track record for significantly improving operational efficiency and security integrity.

o Comprehensive operational expertise includes budgeting, forecasting, projecting, cash and inventory control, as well as security audits pertinent to distribution and merchandising.

o Extensive troubleshooting and problem solving skills in order to rapidly diagnose and remedy operational and organizational dysfunctions.

o Demonstrated interface proficiency with management, key decision makers and affiliated personnel to further organizational policies and objectives.

o Sound analytical decision making abilities supported by seasoned documentation and contract administration.

o Have served as a resource person for new account development, security system analysis and procedure clarification.

o Consistently able to function effectively in pressure situations to meet scheduled deadlines as well as to expediently handle crisis situations.

o Capable of hiring, scheduling, evaluating, training and motivating staff personnel for enhanced performance, productivity and organizational commitment.

o Experience managing large projects as well as multiple assignments simultaneously with emphasis on quality, safety and project integrity.

o Well-developed oral and written communication skills are supported by staff meetings and French facility.

Education

CALIFORNIA STATE POLYTECHNIC UNIVERSITY, Pomona, CA Specialization: Political Science - Pre Law.

MOUNT SAN ANTONIO COMMUNITY COLLEGE, Walnut, CA Associate of Arts Degree: Business Administration.

Professional Experience

ALARM SYSTEMS, Newton, CA
Occupied such positions as Customer Service Manager, Major Accounts Manager, and Central Station Manager. Diverse activities included developing the company's Customer Service Program, Major Accounts and National Sales Departments, requiring policy and procedure initiation, staff supervision and interface with such organizations as Coca Cola, Sav-On, Bullocks, Bergen-Brunswick, and Arrowhead, resulting in an annually recurring revenue in excess of $6 million. Staffed and managed one of the largest and most modern, computerized alarm company central stations. Contributed significantly to the development of a MIS program, providing maximum analysis of customer data, account tracking and management response. Initiated a large scale conversion program, subsequently implemented on a company-wide basis for a savings of $3 million.

Participated in the development of the corporate philosophy and occupied a key role in the Corporate Training Program, functioning as instructor for areas related to Negotiations, Business Writing, Alarm Equipment, Security Policies and Procedures. Participated in top level contract negotiations and legal positioning while boasting the highest customer retention record in the organization. Other activities included troubleshooting and problem solving support to rapidly identify and correct security dysfunctions. Interface with internal API personnel to schedule customer calls and generate effective needs assessments. Provided staff meetings at Corporate offices relative to accounting for all products and services. Also performed budgeting and forecasting. Personnel skills encompassed hiring, scheduling, training and performance evaluations. Authored numerous articles in the company newsletter. Position necessitated strong documentation abilities in addition to effective performance in stressful situations.

THE GROUP, Newton CA

Began with company as a Corporate Auditor responsible for the design, installation and audit of security systems and procedures relative to store operations, shrinkage, inventory control, shipping, receiving, warehousing and distribution. Was rapidly promoted to Loss Prevention and Security Manager with responsibility for directing managers in such initiatives as loss prevention, merchandise control and appropriate documentation procedures for ten branch locations employing over 450 staff personnel. Conducted weekly staff meetings in order to enhance conformance to stated security objectives.

INTERVIEW SKILLS YOU DON'T LEAVE HOME WITHOUT

Casual breeds casualties.

GETTING TO KNOW YOU

Interviews are tantamount to "get to know you" social engagements. If properly handled interviews provide information about problems employers and companies are experiencing. It takes an experienced ear to hear between the lines and spot potential opportunities. Candidates looking for work instead of challenges come across as self-conscious and dependent because they worry how they fit into the existing organizational hierarchy. They listen to themselves talk instead of listening to the employer. When we feel threatened, our listening skills are significantly diminished. When we feel relaxed, we can consider what is being said. Listening allows for strategic responses geared to the present. Discussing ideas and solutions minimizes self-consciousness. You do not need to know all of the problems facing a company. Approaching employers from their self-interest ensures undivided attention and enthusiasm. If the employer likes you and believes you are sincere in wanting to know more about the company, the potential for an offer is quite good.

A psychology professor at MIT suggests a hiring decision can be affected by something as trivial as what we are touching when a decision is made. His research shows decisions can be influenced by the weight of what is being held. An experiment was carried out in which participants conducted mock job interviews. Sometimes the interviewers held heavy clipboards; sometimes light clipboards. When holding heavy clipboards the interviewer was likely to view the applicant as having gravitas. When holding light clipboards applicants were seen as flaky. Our minds take many such physical metaphors literally. In this sense, a business card does not carry the gravitas as a portfolio, something to consider during interviews.

BE PREPARED FOR ANYTHING

It is prudent to expect the best and be prepared for the worst. On the one hand, doing extensive homework prior to an interview can result in never being asked a single pertinent question relative to your research efforts. On the other hand, straight forward interviews can become grueling cross examinations when we arrive unprepared. The more prepared you are the better your chances for displaying confidence. Any inside information about company products and services serves as fuel for discussion. Information encourages confidence. By being prepared for anything your interviewing presentation takes on a relaxed tone. Relaxed interviews yield more offers than tense encounters where both parties experience discomfort.

Some stress is normal. Symptoms of interview stress include irrational thoughts, sweaty palms, trembling hands, muscle tension, memory loss, difficulty concentrating, blushing, obsessive thoughts, hyperventilation and the inability to maintain eye contact. None of the preceding helps fetch job offers. By placing less emphasis on yourself and greater emphasis on problem solving, you learn to channel your stress into productive interpersonal behavior. Systematic desensitization is a therapeutic approach for overcoming phobias and anxiety disorders using cognitive strategies involving graduated exposure. By visualizing and rehearsing your responses prior to interviews, you will learn to overcome fear and avoidance. Rehearsing is crucial when encountering interrogational interviews. Try sitting in front of a mirror and rehearsing interviews and watch how it helps you overcome personal anxiety.

INTERROGATIONAL INTERVIEWS

Interrogational interviews are considered the worst possible experience. They involve a sadistically rapid succession of questions to discover your strengths and weaknesses under pressure. The attempt is to microscopically examine your behavior in an artificially induced, stressful situation can be incredibly unpleasant. Actors and actresses are routinely required to undergo screen tests. The same principle applies to all interviews. There may be more than one person in the room asking the questions. Being prepared with rehearsed lines allows you to come across with confidence and composure. Remain calm and ask questions for clarification and for increasing participation. Rambling responses appear unprofessional. One way to steal time is to restate the question. "I'm not sure I understand what you are asking; could you be more specific?" Show you are undaunted by pressure by slowing the interview. You do not have to have all of the answers. Know-it-alls frequently receive fewer offers because they unwittingly encourage competition.

People talk more than they listen. Word selection and the tone of your voice are all too telling. People with low self-concepts engage in self-criticism and self-doubt. They tend to blame others for their failures. Interviewers interpret low self-esteem as a weakness. It is generally accepted job candidates with high self-esteem speak with confidence. Self-confidence is evidenced by doing and saying what you think is right even at the risk of criticism from the interviewer. Job candidates demonstrating self-confidence learn from mistakes and are willing to take risks to achieve positive outcomes. Low self-esteem becomes evident when job candidates base their behavior on what other people think.

We gain self-esteem when we see ourselves mastering skills and achieving goals through our efforts. Self-esteem encourages us to accept difficult challenges for growth and success. When we are willing to accept difficult challenges, it is communicated through out body language and impossible to overlook by decision makers during difficult interviews.

PHONE INTERVIEWS

The primary objective of a phone interview is to get a face-to-face with a decision maker. One of the strongest attention getters is, "I have an idea." Ideas pique employer interest. The world of advertising preaches the use of the AIDA principle. You can generate employer appetite through Attention, Interest, Desire and Action. The HEART principle involves selling the sizzle through appealing to basic emotions. In short, you can sell Health, Excitement, Achievement, Romance and Treasure. Health is associated with vitality and Excitement through enthusiasm. Achievement is accentuated through your desire to help the company get ahead. Always remember an interview is like courting, and you must be on your best behavior, enjoy people and get along with everyone. Treasure is communicated by ideas which increase profits and decrease overhead.

Phone interviews are much more than talk and passive approaches encourage interrogations. Use tie downs encouraged by Tom Hopkins. Don't ask what day is good for the employer to see you. Ask if Wednesday or Thursday is better. This approach starts the negotiation. Talking more than ten seconds is counter-productive. Rehearse talking in short bursts and allowing the employer to respond. Listen attentively and gauge your response accordingly. Learn to be comfortable with silence.

"I am not hiring at this moment," is an objection which can be overcome. "I can appreciate that and I would be the last person to suggest I can tell the future. However, I would like the opportunity to meet with an expert in the field and introduce myself in case an opportunity avails itself." A little flattery goes a long way. Too much flattery results in a negative reaction. "Send me a resume," is not as negative as it sounds. Respond positively to any offer that affords a next step. "I will be glad to forward you a copy of my resume. And to ensure I do not waste your time, could you tell me what you are looking for in a candidate?" Such a response gets the employer talking again? If the employer states he is too busy to talk or grant an interview, agree with them. "I can appreciate how valuable your time is and I wouldn't ask for an interview unless I was confident my skills and abilities could be of value to your organization. Would it be possible for me to come by and introduce myself the early part of next week?" Professional sales personnel get away with this approach so why can't you? Another response might be, "I can appreciate the value of your time which is precisely why I called. I saved my last employer a great deal of time by implementing numerous method improvements geared to enhancing overall organizational efficiency. I can do the same for you." Rejection is often knee-jerk reactions. The best approach is to use leading responses encouraging additional dialogue in place of "Yes," and "No" retorts. Even if you fail to get an offer there is opportunity to pick the employer's brain and come away with valuable information for use with other interviews. Get the most mileage from every phone call by asking questions.

LUNCH INTERVIEWS

The meal encounter is vastly different than the office interview because a different set of manners and social conventions come into play. In the office, you sit in a designated seat and the roles are clearly defined. Many decisions will have to be made regarding what food you will select, the price, whether to drink alcohol and if you are free to light up a cigarette. On the positive side, the meal interview can mean you are being seriously considered for the job. On the negative side, it casts you in a less formal structure and can reveal things about your behavior the interviewer will use against you in making the hiring decision.

The first rule is to follow the interviewer's lead. Wait until the interviewer is about to sit before taking your seat. Don't force the interviewer to take his seat before you since it may be construed as a power play. If they order a steak, order one also. This doesn't suggest you have to mirror every move. Following the interviewer's lead allows you to select something in the same price range. If they order a drink and you do not drink, order ice tea. If the interviewer orders a bottle of wine, the waiter will inevitably come around to fill empty glasses. It is customary to put your hand over the glass to signify you do not want more. Alcohol encourages a slip of the tongue. Coffee is appropriate, but too many cups encourages a caffeine rush and nervousness. You cannot concentrate when your bladder is complaining.

The first activity after sitting down is to remove the napkin from the table and lay it across your lap. Make sure the water glass is well towards the center of the table so as not to mistakenly tip it over. Tableware is set and used from the outside in. When finished cross your silverware on your plate signifying you are done so the water knows to take your plate away. A book on etiquette will give you more confidence in handling yourself with grace. If the waiter brings the wrong dish or makes a mistake, be humble. The last impression you want to make is being a hard nose. Eat small bites so you can readily respond to questions when asked. Elbows are not placed on the table. Do not get overly comfortable. When the check is delivered, even if it is placed next to you, don't look at it. You are a guest and it is up to the interviewer to pick up the tab. Be gracious in thanking the interviewer for the meal and meeting. Finally, short interviews are better than long ones since a fatigue factor quickly sets in. Being under the magnifying glass is difficult even for seasoned candidates. If more than one company representative is present remain calm, poised and confident.

AVOID NEGATIVES

Never discuss unresolved problems with prior companies. Come up with something positive to say about your last employer, no matter how much it hurts. Do not state something positive only to cancel it out with a negative rider. "I have 120 hours of college but I didn't get a degree". The last part could have easily been left out. "I get along with everyone except my last General Manager." Don't spoil the engagement. The last thing a Ferrari buyer wants to hear is the gas mileage. Emphasize benefits and positive associations! Positive reinforcement leads to positive offers. Clearly state what you can do for a company instead of what you cannot do. If the company asks if you believe you can readily adapt to their fast-paced environment, try the following. "My last company asked the same question. They were surprised at how quickly I started contributing to their projects".

Interviews are opportunities to show we are happy, positive and enthusiastic. The law of attribution suggests we tend to magnify the inadequacies of others and dismiss such inadequacies in ourselves. The tendency to assign more weight to negative information than positive information suggests prejudice, bias and an underlying personality problem impeding adaptation. According to systems theory, the ability to tolerate increased levels of incongruity leads to growth. Negativity and low self-esteem are common bedfellows. Negativity reduces personal and professional energy and costs companies millions of dollars each year. It is an interesting face negative stimuli produces greater neural activity than positive stimuli. Refrain from gossip, complaints and sarcasm which undermine positive energy.

SIGNS OF INTERVIEW RESISTANCE

Feedback is critical for growth and career success. Interviews are rich sources of valuable feedback. Employers are constantly communicating information, both verbally and nonverbally. Avoidance, apathy and silence indicate the employer's interest has not been piqued. Intellectual interviews are not as effective as emotional encounters where feelings are expressed. Intellectualization is a defense mechanism allowing employers to hide their true feelings. Opportunities are incentives which open doors to productive interviews. Instead of emotionally insulating themselves, employers take an open stance and share more about their company when persuaded to talk about themselves. The more information you glean during the interview, the more pertinent your responses.

INTERVIEW JITTERS

When preoccupied with personal needs encounters with decision makers become strained and awkward. To project a willingness to lend a hand, focus on organizational benefits. It is easier to discuss solutions instead of past experiences potentially inapplicable to present organizational needs. Givers gain and undergo productive interviews because the emphasis is on helping instead of taking. The best way to look out for number one is to put others first. "Mr. Johnson, this is what I think I can do for you", translates into, "we against the problem". Change the mood and tempo of the encounter by discussing future developments and applicable changes to foster company growth and efficiency. Begin interviews by telling employers what is in it for them after they make an offer. Ninety-five percent of our clients get better jobs because they have learned the awesome power of appealing to employer self-interest. So can you.

BODY LANGUAGE

It is a fact our attention shifts every four to five seconds so movement is key in maintaining attention. We have all heard the expression "actions speak louder than words." Research shows using confident expressions, body language, postures and assertiveness encourage perceptions of competence and warmth from others. In face-to-face communication, almost ninety percent of the social meaning is derived from nonverbal communication. Cues like eye contact, facial expression and gestures can make a significant difference in the overall impression. Feet shuffling, clenched fist or jaw, crossed arms, voice pitch, breathlessness and frequent speech errors all indicate stress. Rehearse potential responses in front of mirrors and try them on others. Unconscious frowning is the result of being asked questions we find unsettling. The interviewer may not know what is wrong, but arousing suspicion is dangerous.

More offers come with smiles and a little humor. A sense of humor suggests a calm demeanor and confidence when faced with crisis. Frowns intimate attitude problems. A poker face means no interest in the job or no one is home. Eyes have been called the window of the soul because they convey internal feelings. Looking left increases likeability and projects a more relaxed and imaginative demeanor. Looking right communicates a cold, calculating demeanor. Closed eyes suggests temporary flight inwards. Continual eye contact means the need for approval or a challenge. The absence of eye contact denotes retreat. Rapid blinking conveys deceit, disagreement or strong emotional reaction to something said. Crossed feet means being closed to communication and tapping feet suggests inner tension. Outstretched feet convey openness to ideas while feet slipping in and out of shoes demonstrate ambivalence.

Twirling a ring or jewelry is a sign of inner tension and hands obscuring your mouth are taken as the desire to communicate with hesitance or that you are untruthful. Sitting with hands palm up signifies openness to communication. Rapid breathing, deep sighs, clicking of nails and taking glasses on and off translates into tension. Maintaining distance from the interviewer means defensiveness. Sitting next to the door shows the desire to escape. Leaning towards or away from the interviewer denotes confidence or insecurity. A droning, hollow, submissive voice is just as detrimental as clearing your throat and nervous giggles.

Rehearse walking erect with arms and hands relaxed. Imagine a golden thread passing through your spine and connected to a cloud. Again, first impressions include the way you carry yourself. An erect posture suggests leadership and self-worth. Look into employers' eyes when shaking hands, not down at their hand or the floor. Anticipate problem questions and practice making natural responses with sincerity. The inability to maintain eye contact is interpreted as dishonesty or insecurity. When asked a difficult question you know the answer to, practice looking up and to your left to appear intelligent. A pause commands more respect because it looks as if you are thinking before responding. Rehearsal does wonders for creating automatic habits employers will admire.

Don't remove lint from your clothes, clean your fingernails, touch your face or primp your hair during the interview because such actions denote nervousness. It is better to wear glasses than to squint during the interview because you cannot see. Don't apologize for wearing glasses and refrain from taking your glasses on and off during the interview. It comes across as nervous and indecisive. Care should be exercised in selecting the right kind of frames. Certain fashions can make you look younger or older. Avoid granny glasses. Dark glasses suggest you are hiding or taking drugs. Looking over the top of your glasses denotes cynicism. A strap around your neck comes across like as insecure.

Many professionals talk with their hands. It is customary to look at the hands of others while they are drawing you a picture. To avoid staring, occasionally look up and to the left while nodding, as if thinking about what is being said. Wet, clammy hands denote nervousness and arouse suspicion as to why you are so anxious. Maybe you aren't genuine and have something to hide. An old Peruvian story involved a crime with three suspects. A wise ruler had the suspect's hands filled with seed and then bound. The suspects were then placed into a room for the night. The next day the suspects were released and their hands were unbound. Seeds in the hands of one of the suspects had sprouted, indicating guilt. Why? Because nerves cause wet hands, and wet hands in this instance were enough to cause the seeds to sprout. In all cultures wet hands are a sign of nerves. Learn to relax and see how dry your hands become. Shake hands snugly but not excessively. Always shake vertically instead of palm up or down. The customary time allotted to handshaking is approximately four seconds, or four pumps. Do not look down at the hand of the interviewer. Allow the interviewer to establish the cadence of the hand-shake. Over pumping suggests anxiousness and submission.

An even smile is professional. Grinning is adolescent. Tilting the head to one side is a sign of adolescence. Slow head nodding encourages additional dialogue. Fast nodding suggests the need for approval and frequent head nodding indicates excessive eagerness. Professionals cross legs at the knees instead of an ankle across the knee in a horizontal fashion. Never cross ankles. Mirroring, when not overworked, is effective. Leaning inward denotes affinity. Leaning away suggests avoidance. Don't stand with hands in pockets, with weight on one leg, or with ankles crossed. Stand evenly on both feet. Do not rock on the balls of your feet. Walk slowly and deliberately so as to project confidence. Sit only when directed. It is customary to wait until the employer begins to sit before taking your seat. Don't move furniture or sit close to the door as if trying to get away. Always face the employer rather than standing to one side.

ANSWER QUESTIONS WITH QUESTIONS

Listening skills are crucial during the interview. A good listener realizes many questions can be answered with indirect responses. Active listening techniques include summarizing what has been said or asked. Seeking clarification of a question gives more information and allows time to formulate a response. A properly managed interview results in the employer doing most of the talking. Talk is encouraged by nodding, listening, and asking questions about what was said. Behavioral psychologists understand strategic nodding encourages disclosure. If asked an illegal question about age, ask if age is an important factor in making the hiring decision. It serves little purpose to confront the employer with his legal blunder.

Paraphrasing a question shows you are attempting to understand what the interviewer is asking. Passive listening techniques invite interviewers to share more of their feelings and ideas. Responses like, "What I am hearing is;" "This sounds important," "I would like to hear more about that," and "I see," are designed to encourage additional communication. Poor communication skills include being inattentive, jumping to conclusions, interrupting, changing the subject and completing the interviewer's sentence. If asked why you want to work for the company, answer directly and honestly. If asked if you can start immediately do not be overly anxious to reply. "It sounds like you need someone to start right away", would be an excellent response encouraging more dialogue. It is certainly appropriate to ask the person posing questions to be more specific so you do not divulge unnecessary information and lose prestige.

INTERVIEW QUESTIONS AND ANSWERS

Answers are nothing but questions in disguise.

MOTIVE

Questions sometimes have hidden agendas to disclose ulterior motives. Understanding what is actually being asked allows for a satisfying while discouraging additional questions along the same line. When you do not understand the hidden agenda behind what is being asked you ramble, disclose potentially incriminating information, and invite more questions along sensitive lines.

Question: "Why do you want to work here?" The question is designed to uncover motives for seeking work with the company. Are you looking for new challenges or merely a place to get benefits? Do you want to work with a leader or merely have a goal of sending out ten resumes a week to blind companies?

Answer: "I am glad you asked that question. I approached your company because it is a leader in the field of micro-electronics. I have recently undergone training in micro-circuitry utilizing a new photoelectric process. Since your company is involved in similar research, I believe an opportunity exists to apply my training and interest for mutual benefit." This style of response can be applied to any organizational setting and job application.

Question: "Why do you want to leave your present employer?" This is a natural question and effective answers can be rehearsed. Be sure to state your answer in the positive. Stating you want to leave because of inadequate compensation is not as strong as leaving because you are looking for greater challenges to overcome.

Answer: "I am of the opinion a candidate grows in relation to the size of the obstacles overcome. I solved some pretty major problems with my last firm and am convinced I can be of similar service to your organization."

Question: "What elements do you find most interesting about the position?" This question presupposes you have researched the job opening for a fit. The most interesting aspect of any job involves the challenge. Accountants like to balance books. Engineers like making and fixing things. Maintenance engineers like to keep things working smoothly. Managers like to enhance staff efficiency. Sales persons like to open new accounts and territories. Each job niche has its own unique challenges and it is up to the job candidate to find out what they are and exploit them during the interview.

Answer: "I particularly like the fact the company is actively pursuing growth in the market and look forward to being part of a dynamic team. I recently read your engineering department is investigating plastic substitutes for electromechanical parts. My background in plastics seems to mesh well with your future plans and will allow me to immediately begin contributing should you decide to bring me aboard."

Question: "What are you looking for in a position?" This question could mean almost anything. Refuse to lose points rambling. It is reasonable you will be seeking increased responsibility and means for becoming more competent in your occupation. Do not mention you are looking for benefits or similar remarks.

Answer: "I like solving problems and integrating change for enhanced organizational efficiency. I have been of valuable service to my last company and feel confident my skill set can rapidly adapt to your organizational setting."

Question: "What would you like to be doing say three to five years from now?" This kind of question calls for projection. It is also used to test your reality orientation and commitment. If you say you want to be self-employed or independently wealthy, you just put your foot in your mouth. If you say you want the President's position, you might be making a fool of yourself. Play safe, avoid extremes, and go for the central tendency when answering this question.

Answer: "It would be helpful to hear about the kinds of opportunities for upward mobility in your organization." This response prevents the obvious faux pas and puts the ball back in the interviewer's court. If you have a grasp of the potential upward mobility within the company you can give a range of possibilities. Another response might be, "I don't have a specific position in mind at this time; however, I know I will be endeavoring to assume a position of greater responsibility as well as becoming more proficient at solving problems associated with my job description. The satisfaction associated with my ability to contribute is more important to me than an exact title."

Question: "Are you after your boss' job?" This question might be attempting to measure your achievement orientation, an attribute valuable to many companies, particularly those in sales. Ambition is laudable; greed is deplorable. If the interviewer believes you will scratch and claw your way to get ahead, exploiting anyone who can help you satisfy your lust for power and recognition, no offer or recommendation for hire will be forthcoming.

Answer: "I have heard the greatest obstacle to getting a promotion is the lack of a suitable replacement. I would hope my superior would be sufficiently impressed with my performance to recommend me for his position as he moves upward." Such a response shows your motives are sincere and you are a team player. Obviously, the majority of job candidates desire upward mobility because of the additional benefits derived from an increase in salary, prestige, responsibility and influence. To suggest you are not interested in the next position might be taken as a lack of initiative. To be all too eager might project more interest in the next position without sufficient attention to the job at hand.

SELL ME

From the resume through the interview you are always selling yourself. It is quite natural for the interviewer to ask you why you want to join the company. It is also typical for the interviewer to ask you to convince them as to why they should hire you. Your skills and abilities are immediate selling points for potential companies. Never brag, but readily share how you can apply what you have learned and how your troubleshooting competence can readily be used to foster the accomplishment of organizational objectives. No matter what you are asked the real question is why they should hire you. Stick to your qualifications. The more you disclose of your personal nature the less prestige you command because you might distract from the purpose.

Question: "Tell us something about yourself." Don't fall for this opening and digress ad nauseam about your life for the next fifteen minutes while losing points. Generally, the interviewer has something specific in mind in asking such a question. This kind of question may also be posed to encourage job candidates to break the ice, since many job candidates expect the employer to do all the work. Don't forget this is a "sell me" question and places the ball temporarily in your court. The objective, get the ball moving and into the employer's court.

Answer: Using a little disarming humor consider stating the following, "I am confident I could bore you will all the fascinating details of my life for at least the next hour. But in asking your question, I sense you have something specific in mind (smile). Would you care to share that with me?" The ball is now in the interviewer's court. If you rehearsed the response so the correct body language was present, the interviewer complied. If you did not rehearse the response you might have come across as sarcastic. Employers like real people, not those stuffed with self-importance. Productive interviews encompass a range of emotions. A little sense of humor is an important ingredient for productive interpersonal staff relations.

Question: "Why should we hire you?" This question is designed to pull at your ego. Forget impressing them with your bravado and how you graduated first in your class by putting all the other dummies to shame. Some reverse psychology will do nicely and sets a relaxed tone. The question is designed to catch you off guard. Return the favor by giving an untypical response.

Answer: "I would be boasting to tell you what you should (pause and smile), unless of course you are interested in bringing aboard a candidate who can immediately begin reducing operating costs." If the interviewer lacks a sense of humor, you probably would not want to work for the company anyway.

Question: "Tell me why I should consider hiring someone from outside my company when we believe to promoting from within?" Face the reality of the question. If the interviewer could easily hire someone from the inside, they would have already done so. Nevertheless, play the game and give a productive response suited to the question. Confronting the interviewer with a blatant truth is futile.

Answer: "Although companies have recognized the motivational benefits of promoting from within, it is also recognized fresh insights can be realized by introducing new ideas from the outside. I have enjoyed solving a variety of problems for my prior employers and feel I can provide the team with a unique perspective on any problems they face in the future. It should make for a good marriage." This takes care of the question in a positive tone and also markets your skills and abilities as assets to the company. Always attempt to market your skills in response questions posed. Responding to questions is different than declarative statements. The interview is not the time for being subservient and shy. Few get offers when job candidates are unable to communicate their qualities. No one likes to think they are buying wilted lettuce.

Question: "What outstanding qualities do you possess?" We all possess outstanding qualities, but a product response provides the best chance for remaining within the organizational context.

Answer: "I believe my sense of judgment and fairness is close to the top of the list. I strive hard to be fair and consistent in my dealings with peers and subordinates. I also put forth a great deal of effort to analyze problems with particular emphasis on prevention." This opens the door to a better question about your ability to anticipate problems. A professional interviewer seeks to understand underlying motivations through responses to questions. Practice results in more offers and increased compensation.

Question: "Of all your accomplishments which is the most significant?" This necessitates you rank your accomplishments. In doing so, you are making a statement about what you believe to be the most important attributes of the job. For example, getting to work on time is not considered an accomplishment. Troubleshooting and cost reduction are hot commodities. If you reduced costs at your former company talk percentages to pique the employer's interest.

Answer: "I have been so preoccupied with solving problems I haven't really given much thought to my most significant accomplishments. Perhaps the fact I saved my former company two million dollars in operating costs through a major plant reorganization would be considered by some as a major accomplishment. In truth, I believe my major accomplishments are still to come."

FIT

Some questions are actually asking how much do you know about the position and your potential fit. The more you know about a firm the more pertinent your responses. Be ready to respond with your qualifications and expectations to ensure relevance with the existing opening. If the company is looking for someone with a background in marketing, make sure you frame your responses in a marketing context. Avoid disclosing information potentially raising questions regarding your fit. For example, discussing your devoted support of your children might lead a decision maker to conclude you put your child's activities ahead of work assignments.

Question: "What are you looking for in your next assignment?" The real motive for asking this question is whether you are realistic about what the job entails, and whether you are organizationally minded, or comfort minded. Avoid stating you like the benefits, the 40IK car plan, or the pension package. Avoid making benefits obvious or the most important criteria.

Answer: "I thrive on challenges and am looking for opportunities to improve efficiency while reducing waste. I am also looking forward to working with new associates for improved team dynamics and rapport." Discussing what you are looking for in this way informs the interviewer you are seeking increased responsibility.

Question: "Of all the positions you have held, which is the least relevant?" The real question is what you liked least about prior assignments, or what problems you left unresolved. If the new position requires perfection in reporting, stating you did not like the bureaucracy or the red tape of your former position is tantamount to falling on your sword.

Answer: "Perhaps the least relevant position I held was in retail sales. Don't get me wrong, I learned a great deal from my retail assignments, particularly in customer relations. Outside sales is vastly different. It takes more than placing items on a shelf to sell to large companies. I believe my recent sales experience is more indicative of my true potential. As you might have gleaned from my resume, I have been recognized for outstanding sales performance for the last three years in a row."

Question: "How does your experience match this job?" Do you know anything about the company and position offered is the hidden question? If your experience is unrelated, you are not thinking creatively. Speak in terms of similarities.

Answer: "You are looking for a Sales Manager and I have five years' experience satisfying major portions of the job descriptions. Specifically, I have promoted account development for increased revenue and customer satisfaction. I believe my track record shows I am ready to assume the responsibilities expected of a sales manager."

Question: "What do you think are the responsibilities for the position?" This is asking how well you understand the requirements of the job. It is helpful to perform research prior to interviews in anticipation of such questions.

Answer: "I am happy you asked that question. As a production manager, I have successfully set multi-million dollar production back-logs for up to sixty projects simultaneously. This required the ability to route materials through several departments while motivating over 300 production personnel for greater commitment and quality assurance. My job involved interfacing with Engineering, Purchasing and management to fulfill the company's profit objectives. Am I correct in presuming this is the kind of responsibility you are looking for?"

Question: "How will your contributions be different from other candidates?" The hidden question asks how you are different from other candidates, particularly those in house candidates vying for the same position. At this point it is safe to recapitulate your past accomplishments, particularly those associated with being able to solve unique problems.

Answer: "To be specific I would need to know the background of other candidates you are considering. I might suggest I enjoy a reputation for expediency in getting the job done. I am not afraid of challenges and routinely go the extra mile in satisfying assignments. Perhaps you would like to share a little more information regarding the specific requirements for this position so I can give a more precise response."

Question: "How does this position parallel others you have applied for?" What is really being asked is what other positions are you applying for or considering? The question attempts to uncover hidden motives i.e., whether you are talking with a competitor or have other career aspirations than the specialty of the current company.

Answer: "Your opportunity emphasized the need for a seasoned inventory control professional with knowledge of computers. I have a degree in Data Processing and several years' experience developing inventory control programs for my last company."

Question: "How is this position different from your current one?" The real question concerns adjustment. Can you bring to the new position things learned from your last? In short, what areas will not overlap or be transferable? Another aspect of the question might have to do with qualifications i.e., are the positions sufficiently compatible as far as responsibility to warrant serious consideration. Make sure to tie in relevant experience and duties for the employer.

Answer: "Both positions require a Field Engineer with electro-mechanical expertise. What makes your position particularly unique is the emphasis on working in Mexico. I am fluent in Spanish and am looking forward to applying my language skills for improved communication between field projects and the home office."

Stress and Conflict.

Some questions are designed to press your buttons or uncover personality problems in handling pressure situations. How do you approach solving problems? What do you tend to worry about? How do you handle criticism are all questions designed to give the interviewer an accurate picture of your stress profile.

Question: "Tell me how you handle tension?" The real question asks if you can handle tension and stress. Most professionals handle stress through exercise.

Answer: "Admittedly, system programming is a stressful job because we are constantly required to debug complicated software. I have found a major means for minimizing tension is to promote enhanced rapport with working associates and customers. I also like to play racquetball to reduce stress. It keeps me in shape and allows me to maintain mental perspective."

Question: "What do you tend to worry about?" The question could be asking you to identify potential areas of stress about your job, or character weaknesses. For example, if you worry about employee dynamics, perhaps your leadership qualities are insufficient or underdeveloped or your finance acumen is lacking.

Answer: "I do become preoccupied with decisions affecting my job responsibility but by nature I am not a compulsive worrier. Recently a major supplier was undergoing a union strike. We needed raw materials fast. I called alternate suppliers and was able to honor our shipping promises to our customers."

Question: "Can you function in pressure situations?" This is a lead-in question. Be prepared to follow up your response with details about pressure situations. Avoid statements that suggest conflict with staff members.

Answer: "I presently work in a very fast-paced production environment which requires me to make hundreds of decisions on a daily basis. My success in promoting departmental efficiency and reducing staff turnover suggests I thrive on pressure."

Question: "Think of a difficult problem you've recently encountered and what you did to deal with it." The question is attempting to gauge your problem solving and decision making ability. Avoid controversial problems or areas you could have prevented with foresight.

Answer: "I recall making a sales call on a company in Detroit. They wanted to order a larger number of units beyond our manufacturing capacity. I didn't want to lose the sale so I excused myself and made a few phone calls. It turned out we could subcontract the assembly portion of production and fulfill the order. The sale was the largest in the company's history."

Question: "What is the most difficult situation you have ever faced?" This question is a lead-in to others. Be careful in describing difficult situations that might reveal areas of irresponsibility. For example, stating you had a run in with another department chief.

Answer: "I was once required to choose between two highly qualified employees for one promotion slot. Both deserved to advance and I feared the unselected staff member might become demoralized. I talked it over with my superiors. They agreed with my strategy. I convened a meeting with the two employees and asked them for a remedy. They came up with a solution of sharing responsibilities and compensation."

Question: "Describe the last time you and your supervisor disagreed?" This question is looking for personality problems. Can you get along with superiors? Can you take direction as well as give direction? State a positive outcome without anyone losing face.

Answer: "I enjoy a very mature and open relationship with my supervisor. When my supervisor felt one of our employees was causing a major bottleneck in the department I looked into the matter and found the delay was caused by a routing problem in another department. Once I explained the situation my supervisor discussed the problem with the other department head and the problem was quickly resolved."

Question: "Describe the last time you got angry on the job?" Refrain from responses suggesting personal indignation with subordinates or superiors.

Answer: "That's a tough question. I guess the last time I got angry was when one of my colleagues downgraded themselves. My colleague is quite talented and contributes enormously to the company. I don't like it when people discount their abilities. I challenged my colleague with their valuable contribution and they thanked me for it. I would expect the same from them."

Question: "Tell me of an idea you had that was openly criticized?" Make sure you avoid discussing ideas that might be construed as a personality conflict. Again, state something positive.

Answer: "I remember suggesting to the General Manager an idea for reducing the number of union classifications to minimize the rigid job descriptions preventing smooth scheduling. The change would necessitate promoting several workers to higher pay grades. At first, the General Manager thought the ideal was too expensive. Upon closer inspection it became obvious we could actually save a great deal of money because work assignments were more flexible and cross training improved cooperation among workers."

Question: "How do you handle rejection?" Everyone gets rejected once in a while. Avoid feeling sorry for yourself. Show how you took rejection and made it a stepping stone to success. Remember. What we disclose affects the interview relationship.

Answer: "I was once overlooked for a promotion because it was felt I was too young to shoulder the responsibilities of the higher position. At first I felt rejected. I decided to work even harder to prove myself and was soon promoted with an attractive raise in compensation."

Question: "Tell me of a supervisor who was difficult to work with?" This question seeks to understand how you work with authority and what problems you perpetuate. It may be unrealistic to state you never have difficulties since conflict is a way of life in business.

Answer: "I remember working for a Plant Manager who rose through the ranks but harbored an aversion to computers. When sales continued to grow the manager was unable to efficiently coordinate scheduling. I did what I could to provide the necessary support, particularly computer support. With time the manager became quite competent with computerized scheduling."

Question: "When you disagree with your supervisors do you make your opinions known?" The question is, are you a troublemaker who shoots his mouth off when he doesn't get his way. The question also is attempting to assess whether you have the self-esteem to voice your opinions despite the possibility of criticism.

Answer: "I have always felt the best decisions are informed decisions. If I feel my supervisors are not apprised of the total picture I give them the necessary data to make informed decisions. I am happy to report this approach has led to numerous improvements and cost savings overall."

Question: "Why am I feeling you are not suitable for this position?" This question may be designed to measure your composure when confronted with rejection. Avoid taking issue with the question so as to maintain your professional composure.

Answer: "I do not know. Perhaps we have not adequately discussed the needs of the position in relation to my skills and abilities. Can you tell me exactly what kind of qualities you are looking for in a candidate?"

Question: "What interests you least about this position?" This question attempts to identify what reservations you may hold about the position potentially causing conflict after you come aboard. If there are negatives, why are you interviewing? In short, why are you doing them a favor?

Answer: "I cannot say I have seen any negatives at this point. I would like to ask; however, what provisions are there for advancement and what likely positions this slot might lead to?"

Question: "What things did your supervisor do that you disliked?" Whether you like or dislike what your supervisor do, your job is to follow directives to the best of your ability. If you believe a better decision was available, you would confide such information in a tactful way to the supervisor. "Like," in this context, is subjective and business likes to pride itself in objective, critical decision making. If you disclose past problems with supervisors you might be considered a troublemaker or upstart that can't follow orders.

Answer: "I get along well with my supervisors. If there is one area I dislike, it is the fact my supervisor refuses to take credit for anything. This makes employees look like superstars but might not reflect well on my supervisor's true management abilities."

Question: "Couldn't another firm offer you a better opportunity?" This is a negative sell meaning, "Tell me why you want the job." Don't overdo the obvious. Consider why the question is being asked in the first place.

Answer: "I cannot answer that. I like what I see so far. A candidate needs to know when he comes across a good opportunity. I think the fit is right and I look forward to helping your firm if you feel my background compliments your organizational mission."

Question: "What would your response be if I told you your presentation on this interview was mediocre?" This is a stress response test to see how you will react under pressure.

Answer: "Certainly opinions vary but understand I am listening to your comment. I would say I have attempted to convey what I have done for my prior employer and trust you will seriously consider allowing me to apply those same skills to the needs of your firm."

Question: "Tell me the worst thing you have heard about our company?" You can either respond you have not heard anything negative, or state something innocuous. This is no time for true confessions. The interviewer is attempting to identify any misgivings you hold about the job or feels you are taking the position only long enough to find another.

Answer: "Everyone I talk to about your company is positive and thinks it is a good career opportunity. Perhaps the only shortcoming is in the fact you tend to promote specifically from within. I can appreciate your rationale for doing so. I only hope you are aware of the benefits bringing someone in from the outside can provide your company."

OBEDIENCE AND LOYALTY

Some questions are designed to find out about your character. It is reasoned the way you treat your present employer will be projected into the next position. If you take time off during work hours to look for work, the interviewer might consider you are not ethical. Questions can be quite penetrating. The interviewer might ask you about your interpretation of an appropriate length of service. What is they actually are asking is how long will you remain with the company? Questions like this are best answered by drawing attention away from the question itself since there are no exact answers and the interviewer is requesting an opinion.

Question: "You are still employed. How can you interview

under such circumstances?" The question is, "Are you loyal to your company?" Of course you are. Have a positive response available.

Answer: "I have worked a great deal of overtime to ensure my assignments are current. My employer gave me additional time off. Please do not misunderstand me, even though I am devoted to my company I thrive on new challenges and was hoping your company might afford me greater opportunity to exercise my problem solving skills."

Question: "What do you consider an appropriate length of service with a company?" The question is, "Are you going to stay awhile, or will you jump at another opportunity as soon as it avails itself?" Maybe you are, but don't let on as such.

Answer: "I don't have a specific length of service in mind. I trust you will not misunderstand me when I say although length of service is important, it comes in second to results. I have consistently grown in responsibility with each company I have worked for and display a knack for making immediate contributions. And though leaving associates is always sad, I am confident my references will attest to the fact my prior employers benefited a great deal from my dedication."

Question: "You seem to have had a lot of jobs. Why?" Everyone in today's world occupies more positions than the past. It is part of the rapidly changing economy. Don't get defensive.

Answer: "There is no easy answer to your question. I thrive on challenges and contributions of my problem solving skills."
Question: "What other companies are you considering or have made you an offer?" You cannot stop the interviewer from being nosy.

Answer: "Although I would like to share that information with you, I must decline until I have made a firm decision. I will say they share similar attributes with your company, although your firm interests me in particular for the following reasons…"

Question: "May we contact your present employer?" The only legitimate reason they would have for contacting your present employer is to verify your employment.

Answer: "I am sure I can arrange that when the time comes. For the time being, I wouldn't want to alarm my company if they knew I was seeking other opportunities."

Question: "May we contact your references?" If your interview responses were sufficiently convincing, this question may be a matter of form.

Answer: "I have selected several busy professionals who I feel can best reference my unique skills and abilities. Since I do not wish to impose upon their time, I would ask we be close to a decision before they are contacted. Are you prepared to make an offer at this time?"

Question: "When could you start?" Hold on to your seat, the question may be hypothetical and a means to gauge your interest. If you jump in with both feet you might be asked to work for less compensation.

Answer: "I'd like to think I started when I mailed my resume. When do I get introduced to the rest of the team?" As an alternative, "I would like to say right this minute but I am very serious about my commitments. Do you need someone immediately?

Question: "Are you willing to travel?" This question is actually asking if you are willing to go where the company orders you. A lackey will do everything to get approval and typically receives none. Professionals seek to consider opportunities before hastily responding. An affirmative response is customary if you can manage it.

Answer: "I have traveled before and fully appreciate companies need qualified personnel in the field if they are to grow and satisfy customer requirements. I am sure I can effectively represent your firm on any assignments in any area. Do you have an opportunity in mind?"

Question: "Are you willing to relocate?" Like the above question, you are company oriented but need to make informed decisions.

Answer: "My family has become accustomed to using the internet for keeping in touch with relatives. Relocating would largely depend upon the opportunity. If an excellent opportunity is offered, I am confident my family would not wish me to forfeit it. Do you have an opportunity in mind?"

Question: "How well do you take direction?" Corporate dynamics necessitate everyone follows orders.

Answer: "Effective leaders must first learn to follow. I have always prided myself in facilitating organizational policies and procedures and believe I take direction extremely well."

Vitality

Vitality and drive are important elements in hiring decisions. You may be asked to describe a typical day which is a covert way of asking how many hours you work.

Question: "Tell me how your work shows initiative?" This question seeks to know how well you follow through on a plan or task.

Answer: "I enjoy a reputation for anticipating work so it gets done ahead of schedule. I also place emphasis on following through on work assignments and will be happy to provide examples when you have the time."

Question: "How would you describe a typical day at work?" This question is asking how you arrange your work schedule.

Answer: "I arrive at work early and review my assignments for the day to prioritize the most important tasks. A great deal of my time encompasses interfacing with other departments and customers. I have no set time for going home. I stay as long as I am needed."

Question: "What is your greatest weakness?" Since interviews are typically dominated with positive information, some interviewers like to interject a little reality grounding into the dynamics. It is smart to have something innocuous to share when this question arises.

Answer: "Not knowing when to go home might be considered by some as a weakness. I sometimes get so involved with work I forget the time and often have to be chased out of the office."

CONFIDENCE

Confidence scores high marks during interviews. Egomania reduces marketing appeal. Be sure to reference skills and abilities within the company context. When it comes to self-ratings, be conservative and exude quiet confidence.

Question: "How would you rate yourself on a scale from one to ten?" A professor once asked his students what grade they thought they deserved, and then gave it to them. What was alarming was how many said, "C." If you feel you are a ten, say so with confidence.

Answer: "At the risk of sounding conceited, I would give myself a nine and 'needs room for improvement' grade. I am continually striving to improve myself and admit there is always room for improvement."

Question: "How long before you start contributing to the company?" This question sets up a situation where they may attempt to start you off for less compensation on the grounds you need training. Be sure to reinforce the idea you have a reputation for contributing immediately to the forward momentum of the firm.

Answer: "If my last assignment is any indication, I can say immediately with confidence. Within the first month of my employment I initiated three significant methods improvements that saved the company over $500,000 annually. I see no reason why I cannot do the same for your company."

Question: "Have you done all you are capable of doing on the job?" Forget true confessions. If you still have work to do, why aren't you still in there plugging away instead of looking for another position. The basic reason you are looking is because you are looking for new challenges to satisfy.

Answer: "I would like to think I put forth 110%. My main objective as a manager is to remove obstacles in the path of my employees. I am continually looking for ways to improve productivity. This is why I recently took a time management class."

Money

Question: "Your past salary is a little high when compared

with the salary allocated for our position. Will you take less to start?" Becoming indignant or inflexible will only alienate the interviewer. Keep the door open for negotiation.

Answer: "I have never been one to pass up an excellent opportunity solely on the basis of money. What kind of money are we really talking about?

Question: "Why aren't you making more money?" This question is asking about your level of responsibility and suitable compensation. If your salary is low, interviewers might conclude you were not asked to shoulder much responsibility with your last assignment. If so, why?

Answer: "I would be less than honest if I told you I was not interested in money. Money has never been my prime motivation; however."

Decision making

There are several ways interviewers attempt to gauge your decision making competence. You may be asked to explain how you plan and organize a typical day. The real question is what kind of decisions you make. If asked if you can take calculated risks, avoid being overly enthusiastic. Although risks are necessary, companies do not generally encourage them.

Question: "Recall a challenging event. How was your approach different from the ordinary?"

Answer: "I remember being asked to augment production on an assembly line fraught with bottlenecks. I implemented a dual assembly configuration at the beginning of the line allowing crews to jump back and forth as parts arrived. This enabled a smooth transition into final assembly without holding up progress at other stations down line. The line allowed for a 40% increase in unit output."

Question: "What major activities encompass the majority of

your time on during an average day?" This question is looking for wasted time and effort. Can you organize your work schedule? Can you prioritize important tasks?

Answer: "I spend approximately 20% of my time planning, 60% of my time on project management and implementation, 10% of my time on training and 10% of my time on follow-up to ensure plans are effectively communicated and working properly. This ratio seems to work best for me."

Question: "How do you plan and organize for major projects?" The question is how you handle major projects.

Answer: "I utilize a computer to flow chart major assignments to ensure efficient integration of the production. Prior to program implementation, I get department heads involved to ensure we are all working towards the same goal."

Question: "How would you make a decision if no procedure exists?" What is being asked is if you follow company policy or make up your own?

Answer: "I pride myself in maintaining familiarity with the corporate mission and policy manual. I would look for similar problems and decisions. If clear guidelines do not exist, I would make the best possible decision consistent with the overall corporate philosophy."

Question: "From jobs past held, what have you learned?" This is an opportunity to summarize your summary of qualifications with particular emphasis on qualifies most beneficial to the company.

Answer: "Perhaps my most significant awareness involves employee participation and how it facilitates cooperation and commitment. I consistently ask subordinates for their in-put so they feel a part of the decision making process. I attribute this practice with the high morale and low absenteeism in my department."

Question: "Can you take calculated risks when necessary?" Of course you can, but the word, "calculated," suggests you do so with a great deal of information and not capriciously. Be prudent in your response.

Answer: "Although business is risk prone, I would like to believe a great deal of risk can be minimized through careful planning and sufficient data upon which to make an informed decision. When a calculated risk is inevitable, I have proven my ability to be decisive."

Question: "What do you consider the crucial aspects of your job?" The interviewer is looking for a relationship between your last job and the one now offered.

Answer: "My ability to effectively provide for consistent leadership to foster improved performance, productivity and commitment."

EMPLOYMENT

Be prepared to field questions regarding lapses in employment or terminations. Do not volunteer references unless an offer is imminent. You can turn a termination into a positive event if the question is handled properly. You are looking for the right fit and getting a good position is not something managed in a day. It takes effort and talking with many people. You will want to pursue many alternatives.

Question: "Have you ever been fired?" Termination carries fewer stigmas than it once did but still needs to be handled diplomatically. Getting fired because you made a mistake on a project is something you will not repeat if you have learned from the mishap.

Answer: "Fortunately, I have. I say 'fortunately' because being let go helped me tremendously in my future career growth. Without boring you with unnecessary details, I have found there are two kinds of positions in companies; maintenance and innovative. I naively accepted a maintenance position with an organization and could not understand why my creative ideas were continually rejected. I now realize creative innovation is my niche and thrive on positions offering challenges. My former company, by the way, soon went under."

Question: "If your references were asked about you, what would they say?" This is an opportunity to boast a little about your accomplishments and organizational attributes.

Answer: "I would guess they would comment on my dedication to the job and my tenacity for seeing projects through to completion. I have heard through the grapevine my employees like my fair and consistent management style."

Question: "Why haven't you landed a job yet?" Avoid becoming defensive. Getting a job is easy if you are indiscriminate. Professionals choose the right position before accepting an offer which frequently takes more time.

Answer: "I am sure you will agree with me when I say finding the right position is a very serious undertaking. Although I have received offers, it is prudent to make sure there is reciprocal benefit and interest before committing to a position."

Change

Change is everywhere. Those who cannot adapt to change will ultimately fail. Learning to anticipate and adjust to change reflects resourcefulness and competence.

Question: "How has your job changed since you originally joined the company?" In short, has your responsibility waxed or waned?

Answer: "There is a growing emphasis on systems analysis in our department. I recently underwent additional training in programming to successfully create a batch program to monitor quality assurance. Defects are down by 37% since its inception."

Question: "What was the last article or book you read?" Companies like informed workers. Pick something read by most people in your profession.

Answer: Quote something brilliant from the Wall Street Journal or Forbes consistent with the company. Make your selection current. Make a list of publications in your field or the field you are entering.

ACHIEVEMENT

Achievement is something looked for by interviewers. You might be asked how long before you expect a promotion. The interviewer wants to know if you are unrealistic and if he can afford to keep you interested.

Question: "Can you tell me how you moved up through your last company?" Did you stab others in the back? Or were you asked to assume greater responsibility to get things done?

Answer: "My methods are simple. I devote 110% towards every project and place emphasis on working within the corporate mission."

Question: "If brought aboard when would you expect a promotion?" Are you impatient and will you jump to another company if the promotion is not as fast as you expect?

Answer: "I don't have a specific timetable in mind. How do you determine when a person is ready for promotion?"

Question: "What is your opinion of your progress to date?" Are you a rationalizer, or can you do more than you have? Don't share negative information about the lack of opportunity. Sour grapes are ineffective marketing and leave a sour taste in the employer's mouth.

Answer: "I would give myself an incomplete grade. I am growing in competence and still have a lot of work to accomplish."

Question: "Have you ever fired someone?" Some managers feel the easiest means for settling disagreements is to replace the aggravating employee. Nevertheless, the quickest means to mediocrity and financial peril is often to surround you with, "yes men."

Answer: "Unfortunately, I have. I say unfortunately because I believe most workers really want to contribute to the success of the company and that the primary responsibility of management is to remove obstacles getting in the way of employee productivity."

Question: "What kind of people do you most get along with?"

Answer: "Although I tend to get along with most everyone, I especially like people who are consistent in what they say and do." This response implies you are consistent.

Question: "What kind of people do you like least?" Forget complaining about
the case in one particular incident, or workers who show up late. Leaders learn to motivate employee. Are you a leader who had other fish to fry, or a complainer?

Answer: "I tend to get along with most everyone; however, I particularly appreciate honesty and consistency." Avoid phrasing this in the negative.

Question: "What is your greatest strength?" Make the attribute organizational oriented instead of personal so as to maximize employer receptivity.

Answer: "Undoubtedly my people skills is my greatest strength."

Leadership and Teamwork

Although everyone pays lip service to leadership, there are many kinds of managers. Some manage by intimidation while others direct through teamwork. When you describe your leadership characteristics be sure to pay appropriate respect for subordinates.

Question: "Are you a natural leader or a born follower?" Natural leaders are actually both. Leaders anticipate the needs of their followers and remove obstacles in their path.

Answer: "In today's world of work there are no simple lines diving leaders and followers. I enjoy directing others. I also enjoy working to accomplish the directives of my superiors. We all answer to someone. Even the President answers to the Board and follows the corporate mission."

Question: "How would you describe yourself as a manager?" Avoid ego-oriented responses. Rephrase the question so someone else is answering the question.

Answer: "My co-workers would suggest I am an eclectic manager who is capable of multi-tasking. I have successfully demonstrated my ability to increase performance, productivity, and staff commitment. I have also found getting others involved in the decision making process facilitates greater motivation with less organizational resistance."

Question: "How did your last superior get the best from you?" This question is asking how you get the most from your subordinates.

Answer: "I like to be challenged and am team oriented. My last superior valued my judgment and routinely involved me in the major department decisions. I passed along this strategy through my subordinates with equal success."

Question: "Do you prefer working as part of a team or alone?" In short, do you have problems working with a team? Are you a maverick who can't follow company policy?

Answer: "I prefer working both individually and as part of a larger team."

OPINION

Some questions have no exact answers and are designed to test your opinion about certain subjects. Watch for questions that pull at your ego. Conservative answers are better since opinions vary and you never know what the interviewer is really thinking. Just because someone says they do not have a problem with what you say doesn't mean they agree.

Question: "What makes you better than your co-workers?" Replace the term, "coworkers," with, "colleagues," which infers we are not better, just different from one another.

Answer: "I have a slight problem with the word 'better.' I have never felt superior to my co-workers. I pride myself in being a team player who works synergistically with others. I make no excuses for being ambitious, but believe success is a team effort."

Question: "What do you consider a healthy work atmosphere?" In short, the company you are applying to is a healthy atmosphere. Make it obvious.

Answer: "I believe motivation is the by-product of getting

people involved. No one likes to be kept in the dark. The more employees are encouraged to see the big picture the more effectively they can work together. Consistent management reduces employee resistance. This philosophy seems to work for me. What approach does this company take with its employees?"

Question: "On your first day on the job how would you introduce yourself to other company employees?" Do you make demands, or are you a quarterback there to help the team? Professionals take the proactive approach, exercising the initiative to seek co-workers out and introduce themselves. They also act interested in what everyone is doing. They don't ask lots of questions or say how things are now going to be different.

Answer: "I would assure coworkers l am a team player who is there to be of service. I encourage open, honest communication and look forward to being of service."

Question: "In what ways has your work experience prepared you to assume greater responsibility?" How have you grown and what have you learned? Have you been given additional responsibility based on your leadership and initiative?

Answer: "I enjoy troubleshooting and possess profit and loss accountability in challenging settings. I am confident a review of my proficiency for handling a multi-million dollar budgets will show I am ready to confront even greater challenges in my next position."

General Questions:

It is wise to gather information about companies prior to an interview. Background information will include a company's history, key players in the organization and likely competitors facing the firm. Formulate and rehearse appropriate answers in your own words for the following questions:

Why did you leave your last job?

What tasks do you gain the most satisfaction from?
What is a database?
Who is the most important user of a database?
Do you know anyone who works for us?
Where would you really like to work?
Can you describe yourself in one word?
What type of books and publications do you read?
Why did you choose your specific university?
What would you have done anything differently in your life until now?
What career goals have you set yourself?
What influenced you to choose this career path?
What do you know about our company?
Can you think of any improvements to our products and services?
What changes would you make in our company if I hired you?
What was the biggest challenge you have ever faced?
Describe a situation where you arrived at a compromise with a colleague.
Can you give examples of your adaptation to diverse peoples?
Which areas of the world would you like to explore and why?
Can you give an example of your multi-tasking skills?
Have you ever considered starting your own business?
What significant contribution did you make in your previous company?
Could you have done better in your previous job?
What would you like to improve professionally about yourself?

Ask questions:

Intelligent questions add points to the interview and increase participation and cooperation if properly phrased. Do not be subservient. Marketing implies an exchange of services. The more information you have the more intelligent and informed a decision you can make.

Why is this position open?
How long has this position been open?
How many candidates have applied for this position?
Are company employees also applying for this position?
Can you tell me the average turnover for this position?
Do you have a timeline on when the hiring decision will be made?
What is the exact job description for this position?
Where the job located and what are the travel requirements?
To whom would I report and will I get to meet his person?
What other departments would report to the position?
Can you tell me how the department is structured?
What would my first assignment entail?
Will I be encouraged to learn about the company beyond my department?
What kinds of training am I expected to undergo?
What are the first projects to be addressed?
What are the major problems to be confronted?
What is the corporate mission and philosophy?
What approach does your company take in the marketplace?
How are the functions of the department recognized by upper management?
What potential career paths in the company will be available?
What opportunities for growth are possible for this position?
How do you determine when a person is ready for promotion?
Who will the company's major competitor be over the next five years?
Does the company have plans for relocation, expansion, or

closings?

Are sales going up, coming down, or remaining the same as last year?

What are the company's strengths compared to the competition?

Could you explain the corporate structure?

What skills and abilities are prerequisites for getting ahead in the company?

Who will be performing staff performance evaluations?

How regularly do evaluations occur and what criterion do they follow?

What personality traits are considered critical for this position?

How much autonomy will I have on my first assignment?

How do you see me complementing or facilitating the group?

What is unique about how this company operates?

What new systems or procedures have recently been implemented?

Can you describe an ideal employee?

THE FOLLOW-UP

The follow-up begins before you leave the interview. Ask for a business card and about the next step in the hiring procedure. Ask if you can connect on LinkedIn after the interview. A follow-up letter or note after the interview reinforces the employer's memory and shows sincere interest in the position. Consider carrying a pack of postage cards and scribbling thank you notes on the back when leaving the company. Conveniently drop it in the nearest mail box so the employer gets it the next day. Less than 3% of job candidate's follow-up on interviews. Why send out resumes and attend interviews only to drop the ball when you might still in contention? If the employer is sitting on a stack of resumes your note could move you to the top of the pile. It is not what we do wrong, but what we fail to do right which typically prevents offers. Using the follow-up beats 95% of the other candidates lacking foresight. Interviews involve talk but do not necessarily indicate action. Follow-up notes show action and sincere interest in the position.

DISPARAGE NOT

Although qualifications are important, offers result from developing personal relationships with employers. There is no precise set of rules for separating one candidate from another. The main ingredient is charisma. Employers appreciate help and support. Beware of questions like, "Why did you leave your last job?" Disparaging your last job or employer is the quickest means for undermining employer confidence. The television movie, "Star Trek", placed strong emphasis on loyalty and camaraderie. Company offices are metaphorical bridges. Personal achievements are less important to most companies than positive staff dynamics.

Leaving your last company must be positively portrayed to minimize stigma. Staff reorganizations raise questions. Why were you laid off? Were you a marginal team player? Were your sales commissions down? Inform potential employers you are looking for new and greater challenges to minimize conversations about former employers. If strongly encouraged to disclose something negative, state growth was minimized. This is a stronger statement than declaring you could not learn anything new. Learning suggests training, and training translates into reduced compensation. Companies pay more for job candidates who can contribute as soon as their feet hit the floor.

THE GOLDEN MEAN

Over 2,000 years ago, the Greeks proclaimed moderation as the secret ingredient for a successful and satisfying life. Their philosophy goes double for career development today. The Golden Mean is the desirable middle between two extremes. An over emphasis on strength or weakness impedes offers because employers reject deviations from the mean. Making the company measure up to your expectations or qualifications is unrealistic and comes across as arrogant. Personal strength is best demonstrated through ideas. Salty language or bawdy jokes may cause laughter on the outside while hiding contempt on the inside. Over dressing or under dressing distracts from the interview.

Jewelry, hair, make-up, posture, and attitude can encourage or deter offers. Assume a conservative approach and see offers follow. Sitting in a military fashion encourages a guarded interview. Relaxed encounters allow employers to disclose what they are really looking for in a candidate. More deals are made on the golf than in the office suggests relaxed encounters are more productive. Employers like employees who allow them to relax over those who force formality. Creative problem solvers might consider inviting decision makers to play a round of golf to discuss ideas for helping companies achieve mission objectives. Why not think outside of the box?

HOW TO CLOSE

An interview is a sale and the strategies employed to get job offers is no different than the strategies used to close consumers. A close is generally the point where both a customer agrees to buy. In a hiring context, the close is where the employer asks when you can start. The secret to a successful close it to emphasize mutually beneficial relationships promising to make the company more successful in achieving its goals. At every point during the interviewing process the job candidate is ensuring a mutual understanding and clarity on how the job candidate can provide value to the organization. During the discovery phase prior to sending resumes, job candidates ensure their background matches the needs of the company. During the prospecting phase the job candidate investigates information about the company to show they have done their homework during the interview. During the listening phase or the interview, job candidates develop greater understanding of what the company needs and hopes to achieve. The closing stage is where job candidates elicit employer appetite so offers become imminent.

Leave interviews on a positive, dynamic note to etch presentations in the minds of employers. "Where do we go from here" is unimaginative and lacks impact. Summarizing potential company benefits is a powerful technique. Recalling employer comments during the interview demonstrates listening skill and interest. Be bold. If employers ask when you can start, ask when they need someone to come aboard. "I look forward to hearing from you" is not as positive as "I look forward to being of service." Within five minutes employers make a favorable or unfavorable impression and changing their mind is nearly impossible. Assumptive closing means you presume you already have the job. If benefits were correctly portrayed, acting as if you are already on board shows initiative and confidence. Interpersonal psychology teaches you may not always get what you want, but you generally get what you expect.

EMPHASIZE SIMILARITIES

Similarity refers to how closely attitudes, values, interests and personality match between job candidates and organizations. A client wanting to make a career change from interior design to industrial engineering read everything in the library dealing with the field. Prior problem solving was then applied to manufacturing using proprietary terminology. The client practiced in front of a mirror and with supportive friends to become proficient with the industrial jargon. When the client recounted their experience during the interview they translated their experience into industrial jargon. By emphasizing similarities, the client came across as an insider instead of an outsider. The client received an offer from the first company they interviewed with because similarities were emphasized. Arbitrators have encouraged common ground discussions for years because the approach works.

No matter how disparate the views of both parties, the first step is to see what both sides have to gain. When discussing prior experience preference is given to elements similar with the position sought. Reduce the likelihood of being asked to take less compensation by discussing solutions. Companies pay less when they can justify additional training during the transition. Market yourself as a general problem solver who can immediately begin contributing to the success of the organization. Show how with each subsequent assignment your competence grows.

SUCCESS IS BEING OF SERVICE

The path to greatness is through the door of social responsibility

BALANCE

Emotional balance happens when everything fits together harmoniously with an absence of stress. Studies suggest more than half of all employees experience high levels of conflict between work and family. If your effort to be of service is costing you more than you can afford in terms of your physical, mental and emotional well-being, it is time to change jobs. Hegel suggested life is in continual flux. Aristotle suggested the greatest virtues are those which are most useful to others. Being of service can harmonize the physical, mental, and emotional dimensions of our lives allowing us to successfully arrive at the fourth dimension called transcendence as illustrated by the psychologist, Maslow. Transcendence involves an integrated life style. Working in the correct organizational climate can go a long way towards fostering transcendence. Wanting to get up for work in the morning is self-actualizing and finding the correct environment from which to launch your specialized skills and abilities is critical to peace of mind and growth. Having responsibilities is highly motivating because someone depends on us. Being asked to mentor fellow employees bolsters confidence and self-worth. Charisma results from a balanced life-style. When participative actions become congruent with thoughts, offers are attracted because interviewers sense integrity. When preparing for a job interview, practice closing your eyes and taking deep breaths through the nose and holding it for as long as possible before exhaling through the mouth. With practice this process allows for deep relaxation, lowering the tone of your voice and exudes poise and confidence when interacting with others.

PHYSICAL FITNESS

The Journal of Occupational and Environmental Medicine shows works who engage in moderate exercise have higher work quality and better performance. An interesting study in Copenhagen found men with low physical fitness are at increased risk for cardiovascular mortality from working long hours. Exercise, a balanced diet and fresh air are the secret to health, wealth and vitality. We are currently experiencing a health revolution across the nation with jogging shoes being refined through sophisticated research and technology. Our entire attitude about appearance is being altered. Physical fitness results in stamina and vitality, both of which are communicated during the interview. Coffee and doughnuts are insufficient ingredients to get up for an interview. Energy is communicated on a deeper level. Consistency is a quality looked for if required to undergo multiple interviews with organization.

Exercise improves mood and brainpower while reducing stress. A number of studies point to reduction of illness, relief from boredom and pent up aggression, and lower absenteeism in workers who exercise. Vitality is energy and vigor communicated through body language, speech patterns, skin tone, and eyes. Work requires discipline, and physical conditioning suggests to employers you possess control in other areas as well, like having the stamina to put in additional time to follow through on assignments. Abusing sugar and caffeine encourages a quick lift followed by a swift drop in energy. Sugar provokes stress, and not fitting into your clothes diminishes self-esteem and marketing appeal. Smoking reduces oxygen to the brain resulting in nervousness and irritability, not to mention the odor that sticks to our hair, clothes and teeth. Breath mints imply an attempt to hide something worse, like alcohol. Protein is a good energy source when combined with vitamins and minerals. Carbohydrates are important for sustained energy. A balanced diet in conjunction with exercise fosters vitality and well-being. Do today what feels good tomorrow. Salads, fruits, and fruit drinks are excellent energy sources prior to interviews. Excessive quantities of meat encourage sluggishness. Food has calming properties. Eating prior to interviews assists relaxation. Unsupervised crash diets leave us weak and demoralized.

HYGIENE

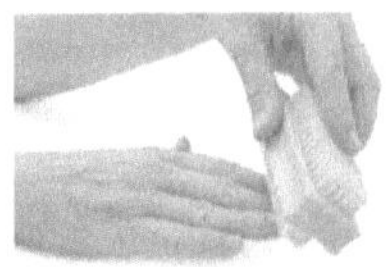

All the effort to mail resumes and attend interviews can quickly be sabotaged by inattention to hygiene. Good hygiene is known to prevent illness and enriches interpersonal dynamics. Skin problems have been associated with not keeping hands clean. Hygiene is critical to offers. Excessive after shave or perfume is overpowering. Cigarette smoke is no longer tolerated. Gum chewing gum comes across as nervous and adolescent. Fingernails should be trimmed and clean. Men can get fingernails white prior to an interview by soaking them briefly in a weak Clorox solution. Trimming nasal hair is a must. Interpersonal psychology teaches face hair, no matter how manicured, generally puts distance between the candidate and employer. Long nails suggest greater concern with fashion than work. Moderation is the key. Prevent looking like Genghis Khan by trimming nose hair. It is not what we do wrong but what we fail to do right that prevents offers. Touch all the bases for confidence in appearance. Hygiene must not become a distracting element.

CHANNELING FEAR

Fear can be identified in three stages: First is the activating incident. Second is the belief system. Third is the way we react to the incident. By identifying what causes fear we can investigate our feelings towards an incident and then select better ways of reacting to it to reduce a negative response. It is understandable to experience butterflies during interviews. The solution is to make them fly in formation. Need for positive regard means we may become overly sensitive or influenced by the attitudes and expectations of others. State your convictions confidently during the interview and understand total acceptance is unnatural and unrealistic. The greatest obstacle to an effective interview is fear of the unknown which quickly translates into self-doubt. Temporary unemployment has been sown to erode self-esteem. To minimize anxiety, channel fear into areas fostering confidence. Exercise causes a surplus of endorphins in the brain contributing to a sense of well-being. Exercise reduces apprehensiveness. If temporarily unemployed, physical exercise cannot be overemphasized. Breaking into an exercise sweat prevents sweating through an interview. If coupled with a balanced diet, and preparation, interviews encourage feelings of strength, relaxation and control.

FEAR OF FAILURE

Fear of failure stops us from moving forward to achieve our goals. Symptoms of atychiphobia include low self-confidence, xenophobic reluctance to try new things, procrastination, and failure to follow through on goals. Unfortunate side effects associated with being unemployed or underemployed include depression and disillusionment. When we question our skills and abilities we begin considering jobs below our capability. It is important to put failure in perspective. Walt Disney was once fired from a newspaper because he lacked creative ideas. Albert Einstein did not learn to read until the age of seven. Charles Darwin was a medical school dropout. Winston Churchill was defeated in every election for public office until he became Prime Minister at the age of sixty-two. Fred Astaire flunked his screen test with MGM. The Harry Potter author, J.K. Rowling, went from living on welfare to become a successful writer. Michael Jordan was cut from his high school basketball team. Babe Ruth struck out 1330 times at bat. Before Akio Morita founded Sony, he failed at selling rice cookers. Failure is frequently a stepping stone to success when we persistently follow our vision.

PSYCHOLOGICAL CRABS

Crabs attempting to escape from a bucket will be pulled down by other crabs in to the bottom of the bucket. This example refers to people who discourage ambition by denigrating ideas for getting ahead. Human crabs have subtle methods for keeping your growth and dreams at a minimum. Blockers are crabs who openly negate anything and everything. Blockers are conditioned to thinking in terms of why things won't work. They refuse to see possibilities. Interpersonal psychology teaches projection is when people insert their own fears and shortcomings into the lives of others. Blockers justify their lack of progress by convincing others they need to stay put. Using Blockers as sounding boards results in demoralization. Ideas work because they are backed by confidence and effort. Prevent negativity and disillusionment by staying away from psychological crabs. Asking green-eyed friends for career advice is tantamount to occupational suicide. Reflect on major decisions of past. Did friends encourage or undermine proposed ideas? If the latter, avoid contact with depressive personality types when important decisions must be made.

POSITIVE AFFIRMATIONS

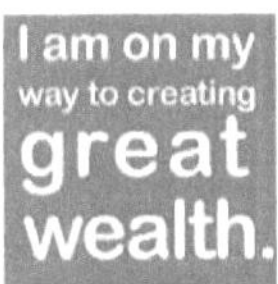

Interpersonal psychology teaches what actually happens is not as important as what is perceived to have happened. Situations are reacted to improperly because faulty perceptions and anticipations bias outcomes. Our actions dictate reactions from others. A way of ensuring our actions are positive is to employ positive affirmations. Creating and posting positive affirmations on walls, mirrors and refrigerators elevates motivation. Each time a positive affirmation is read it is programming into the unconscious mind. Thoughts change behavior, just as behavior changes the way we think. If you harbor an aversion to interviewing, post an affirmation on your bathroom mirror stating, "I love interviewing." Positive affirmations facilitate the development of positive attitude towards life. Positive affirmations turn failure into success and take success to a higher level. Try practicing a technique advocated by the physician Emile Coue. Recite, "Every day in every way I get better and better," every morning and realize the new power you commend over your job search and subsequent interviews.

PASSIVE AGGRESSION

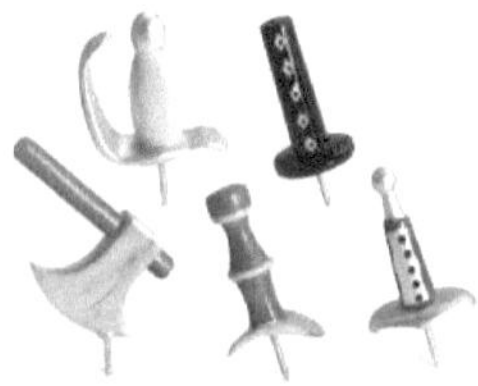

Anger has been called the wind that blows out the light of the mind. Passive aggression is expressing anger in a non-assertive, subtle manner. When unable to confront a situation directly, or unable to fulfill a wish or need, resentment gives rise to inappropriate thoughts, feelings and actions. When we feel incompetent, unappreciated or unable to make decisions, passive aggression rears its ugly head. Fear of competition in an interview can lead to passive-aggressive responses where job candidates sabotage interviews.

Examples of passive aggression include sarcasm, procrastination, excuses, being stubbornly unhelpful, withholding important information, complaints of boredom, scorning authority, arguing, pouting, creating confusion, and cancelling interview appointments. Unconscious resentment discourages offers. Asking every employer to value our skills and abilities is good marketing; expecting them to value our skills and abilities is unrealistic.

PREVENTING DEPRESSION

Interpersonal psychology teaches depression is associated with worry and fear. Symptoms of depression include fatigue, guilt, difficulty concentrating, restlessness, irritability, agitation, lack of interest, feelings of helplessness and hopelessness. Since depression is a common experience when in between jobs, it is recommended job candidates get involved in group activities and consider volunteer positions to maintain a feeling of self-worth. Helping others sustains self-confidence. Through exercise, positive affirmations, market research and willingness to help others, depression is significantly alleviated. Affiliate with people who are positive and caring. Anyone not supportive of your occupational ambition is to be avoided. A few minutes with a negative personality can undo weeks of hard-earned confidence. Avoid reading negative news. Without faith, your chances of getting a really good job are minimized. Cultivate friends and associates who want you to succeed.

REJECTION

The need for acceptance and caring interpersonal relationships causes the adoption of a social personality. When job candidates interview for a job, the process involves gaining acceptance from the interviewer in the form of an offer. Social identity is an important element impacting self-esteem. When we are accepted we feel good about ourselves. When we are rejected we experience interpersonal anxiety. An interesting experiment involved a group of three people tossing a ball to one another. Two of the participants were secretly directed to stop tossing the ball to the third participant after a few tosses to gauge the excluded person's reaction. Without exception, the third participant experienced negative emotions ranging from anger to sadness.

Feeling rejected when interviews do not convert to job offers can lead to withdrawal and depression. It is important for job candidates to remember career marketing is a numbers game similar to other marketing programs. Consider the number of consumers bombarded by ads, direct mail, commercials and telemarketing calls who never purchase a product or service. Several doors may need to be opened prior to finding the right job opportunity. Rejection means the company doesn't have problems which complement your specialized skill. Never allow your self-esteem to deteriorate. Interpersonal psychology teaches lack of reinforcement and praise leads to self-doubt underscoring the importance of considering job clubs and networking. We habitually place emphasis on what others think; a process called conditional regard. The most important regard is how we feel about ourselves. Forget what others think. People tend to take us at the value we place on ourselves. Employers are less inclined to reject ideas on how they can resolve their objectives faster, cheaper and with less difficulty. Create interview incentives and receive more offers. Believe in yourself. Not getting an offer translates into, "Next."

GOALS

Without vision we lose our ability to navigate towards important goals and objectives. Self-actualization stems from the successful pursuit of goals. Growth lies outside of our comfort zones. Lives of quiet desperation are founded on "settle for" attitudes about work. A salary alone is insufficient to sustain motivation and happiness. If we love our job we will never have to work again because happiness is not work. Job satisfaction is a growing demand among workers. A wise mentor once taught the importance for having lofty ambitions; "To shoot at an eagle might result in hitting a rock. To shoot at the sun might result in hitting an eagle." Shoot high and dare to dream! Almost without exception, successful professionals demonstrate persistence in pursuit of their dreams. They etch the vision in their brains.

The psychologists, Alfred Adler advocated Fictional Finalism; the belief fictional goals guide present behavior. Goals are critical to our mental health and objectives reduce confusion. Set specific goals regarding the number of interviews you are willing to go on and the kind of job you want. Getting what we want grows from worthy ambitions and commitment. If working, one interview a week might be all there is time for. If between jobs try to schedule at least five interviews a week. With practice successful job candidates strive for several interviews a day to minimize travel requirements; particularly with out of area opportunities. Wanting a better job is a worthy goal, but too general. Setting a specific job goal defines occupational boundaries and simplifies the job search. Focus job searches on specific areas. Napoleon concentrated all of his artillery on one spot to break through enemy lines with his artillery. Approach local companies first to minimize the inconvenience associated with commuting.

BELIEF

When we find ourselves in between jobs, we experience social exclusion because we are temporarily blocked from opportunities and resources afforded those who are working. In modern societies paid work is not only the principal source of income, it also provides identity and feelings of self-worth. Work is a social network providing a sense of being embedded in society. Being marginalized gives rise to feelings of alienation. Research has shown social rejection activates the same areas of the brain as physical pain.

The link between thoughts and behavior is well documented. Thoughts lead to changes in behavior. Changes in behavior lead to a changes in our beliefs. Belief in self precedes an ability to convince others to believe in us. Belief requires the expectation actions will lead to positive outcomes. Gandhi said we are the center of a circle without a circumference. We determine our limitations because of limited thinking. We only need to be right 51% of the time to be successful. Failure and indecisiveness are bedfellows. Fear of failure leads to reduced performance. Interpersonal psychology teaches there is a silent observer in the unconscious mind working to support our beliefs. If we think in terms of limitations the silent observer encourages failure. When we think in terms of success the silent observer works hard to bring about prosperity. This mental thermostat is critical to our career results.

A manufacturing engineering novice was asked to create a specialized alignment fixture only someone with years of experience could do. Instead of thinking failure, the engineer went into the factory and asked those directly involved with aligning parts what they expected the new fixture to accomplish. Not long afterward the engineer amassed sufficient information to design the fixture. Learn to ask questions so your ideas are congruent with the needs of the organization and are subsequently endorsed by the people you work with. Participation generates greater cooperation than expert approaches to problem solving.

30 DAYS TO A MORE SUCCESSFUL CAREER

The foundation of tomorrow's success is built today.

SOCIAL INTEREST

The psychologists Shannon and Guerney found when we approach others with advice, they respond with cooperation and rapport. When we approach others with competition, they respond with reciprocal competition and aggression. When we approach others from a position of subservience, others respond with domination. This research recommends approaching employers with a willingness to help them solve problems so employers will cooperate with our desire to come aboard.

Social interest is a useful yardstick for measuring psychological health. Virtually all civilizations have a golden rule. Committing the rule to habit encourages benefits beyond comprehension. The strongest truth shows others will gladly give to get. This philosophy requires we put others first. Help yourself by helping others get what they want. Convenience stores operate on the principle of immediate gratification. Price is not the dominant consideration. Similarly, compensation is not the prevailing element in the hiring decision. Making the employer's job easier goes a long way towards getting an offer and receiving elevated compensation.

SUCCESSFUL CAREER STEPS

The first step in finding the right job is to choose a career field. A resume is then created using applicable skills and abilities pertinent to the requirements of the field. Make a list of potential companies who might be persuaded to grant an interview once their interest is piqued by your resume and cover letter. Make the effort to investigate the chosen career field to identify potential opportunities. The chances of getting a good offer increases exponentially with the number of people approached. It may be profitable to take a position temporarily while looking for a better opportunity to keep desperation at bay. Cultivate a willingness to serve others. Make it a habit of visualizing potential solutions to problems employers face. Enlarge your wealth consciousness. Interviews are fun and reinforcing once questions can be responded to proficiently. After amassing a comfortable nest of offers, leverage them into a handsome compensation package with the most desirable company.

Leaders are adept at summarizing the wants and needs of others. Leaders serve as vessels to help others achieve expectations. Leaders act instead of react to their environment. Leadership is taking control of a direction in life. No one holds the only answer to career fulfillment. At best, experience helps in the clarification of career aspirations. Career decisions are subjective. When you perform an inner assessment, consider what field and opportunities are of interest and how you can become of service. Helping companies solve problems is fulfilling and generates enthusiasm for the job.

LESSONS ON DRESS

In discussing dress it is important to understand the psychology of color. An interesting research study involved washing detergent. Consumers were mailed three washing detergents to evaluate. What they did not know was it was the same detergent in three separately colored boxes. Consumers thought detergent in the red box too strong. Detergent in the blue box was too weak. Detergent in the red and blue box was considered just right.

Black is the color of power, stability, strength and authority. White is generally associated with creativity, cleanliness and purity. Blue is associated with calm, wise, loyal, steady and dependable. Green is associated with wealth, harmony, support and nurturance. Red is associated with energy, excitement and movement. Gray is associated with practicality.
Yellow is associated with happiness, optimism, and creativity. Brown is associated with stability, friendship and reliability. Purple is associated with wisdom, wealth, sophistication and prosperity. Color is behind how we dress, speak, write, design, and present proposals. The strategic use of color can influence perceptions.

FORMAL DRESS

Tie shoes are more formal than loafers and black shoes more formal than brown. A blue suit projects greater authority than gray, or brown, just as a white shirt commands more respect than a colored one. Button collars are more casual than plain collars, and ties should be selected with conservativeness and color blend in mind. Candidates coming before a Board of Directors wear blue, pin striped, three piece suits, white, plain collar shirts, black tie shoes with French toes, and blue striped conservative ties. No collar pins, stick pins, tie clasps, flowers, handkerchiefs, fraternal buttons, or earrings that could unfavorably bias employers.

Socks should match shoes or pants and come up to the calf in case legs are crossed. No briefcase. Instead, a 9x12 leather folder is brought along with a copy of the resume and references inside. Hair does not look just cut and no western length sideburns. Pinkie or fraternal rings, like other unnecessary accessories, unfavorably bias employers. A gold watch with a leather band shows class. Bulky skin-diver watches do not. The higher the salary sought, the more subtle the attire.

INFORMAL WEAR

Appearance can be toned down to a softer look by wearing two piece gray or brown suits. Pastel, button collar shirts, conservative ties and loafers also project relaxed confidence. Other accompanying items remain the same. If a suit is too strong for the occupational profile as might be the case for some hands-on field positions, a conservative sport coat with a possible V-neck sweater would work. Stay away from belts with large, loud buckles. Money spent on quiet accessories offends no one. Only youngsters carry wallets in back pockets. Of course, artists might get away with sport jackets, jeans and tennis shoes. This dress is not for everyone, obviously.

LADIES DRESS FOR SUCCESS

Suits and dresses are appropriate attire for the business world and professional women undergo color analysis to discover hues that look best on them. Competing against males, women find it helpful to go formal. A dark suit similar to what Stewardesses wear is an example of professional, formal attire. Hosiery conforms to natural skin tones. Overpowering perfume, loud lipstick, and excessive make-up reduces presentation. The continued emphasis is on quiet elegance. Basic business colors for women include navy, black, camel, gray, brown, taupe, wine, bone and ivory. Secondary colors portray femininity and encompass clear, muted or pastel in such hues as red, yellow, teal, royal, peach and pink. Basic colors portray seriousness and authority. A basic colored outfit can be enhanced through the strategic use of secondary colors. No sandals or slides. Acceptable shoe styles include open toe with closed heels, closed toe with sling heels, and closed pumps. Shoe color matches 80% of clothing. Shoes are polished and heels repaired.

Jewelry is tasteful. Avoid bangles and large necklaces. Notebooks are more elegant than briefcases. Briefcases look foreboding, like you brought along the kitchen sink or need supporting documentation. Why encourage interrogations? Too many curls or hair puff reduces professionalism. Cleavage and short skirts make it difficult for employers to stay on purpose.

HOW TO FIND INFORMATION ABOUT COMPANIES

There are literally hundreds of sources holding critical information about companies. Sales, products, policies, what others say about them, and Government statistics are all included. The more you know about a given field, the more confidence you will have during the interview. Many publications offer SIC (Standard Industrial Classifications), a four digit number that can help you pinpoint what the company does.

Annual Business Reports.
Bloomberg News Service.
Business Information Sources,
Business Organization and Agencies Directory,
Business Periodicals Index,
Business Week,
California Manufacturers Register.
Breaks down companies by name, geographical area, product and service,
Career Employment Opportunities Directory.

Useful for looking up information about specific career fields,
Career Opportunities Index,
Census or Population (Government Statistics).
Population counts can indicate areas to apply valuable services,
Census of Business (Government Statistics),
Census of Housing (Government Statistics),
Census of Manufacturing(Government Statistics),
Chamber of Commerce Directories.
Use to obtain specific information about local Chambers. Each Chamber lists local companies as well as valuable operating information,
Contacts Influential.
Corporate reports.
Companies geographically correlated with phone numbers and important decision makers,
Dictionary of Occupational Titles,
Directory of Career Resources for Women,
Directory of Corporate Affiliations.
Find out who is affiliated with whom so as to interview with added leverage. Can supply
additional leads,
Directories of Directories,
Directory of Executive Recruiters,
Dun and Bradstreet.
Encyclopedia of Associations,
Encyclopedia of Business Information,
Executive Employment Guide,
Federal Career Opportunities.
Useful if looking for a government job. Information about prerequisites.
Forbes.
Fortune Magazine.
Fortune's Plant and Product Directory.
Guide to American Directories.
Handy master research guide for identifying other directories

you may want to research,
Guide to Occupational Exploration,
Hoovers.com for information about 65M companies.
Kelly's Manufacturers and Merchants Directory,
Lesis/Nexis for news stories about companies.
MacRae's Blue Book.
Measuring Markets (Department Of Commerce),
Moody's Industrial Manual.
Multinational Marketing and Employment Directory,
North American Securities Administrators Association.
Places Rated Almanac.
Gives valuable information about Standard Statistical Metro-
politan
Onesource.com to identify key executives.
Areas useful when considering a relocation,
Poor's Registry of Corporations,
SEC database known as EDGAR.
Statistical Abstract of the United States,
Standard Periodicals Directory.
Standard and Poor's Corporate Profiles.
Good resource for locating periodicals regarding specific occu-
pational areas,
U.S. Industrial Directory,
Wall Street Journal Index,
Who Owns Whom.
World Wide Web search via Google, Bing, Infoseek and thou-
sands of other engines.
You might want to send your resume to the Parent company in-
stead of a subsidiary,
Women Helping Women: State Directory of Services,
World Wide Chamber of Commerce Directory.

POST SCRIPT

Change is best and quickest when we personally see the need for it. Increased compensation stems from the level of service we render others. Launching our skills in a corporate vacuum is counterproductive. The psychology of interpersonal success is founded upon a simple rule: Before employers care how you feel, they have to feel you care. Caring is best experienced through a willingness to solve problems facing others. Review your skills and attitudes with an eye for how experience and qualification can be converted into problem solving strategies. The adage, "Use it or lose it," translates into lost opportunities because we waste our potential on uninteresting jobs leading to moribund brain death. Ideal positions stimulate creative thought and commitment so we are motivated to put forth greater effort in helping the company. Our efforts are rewarded with higher compensation because of our contributions. The idea it takes money to make money is based on the reinforcing qualities of increased compensation. The more we make the more motivated we are to achieve higher ambitions. Psychology teaches confident workers readily gravitate to larger and more complex problems. Want more money and excitement in work? Find a company facing a sufficient number of challenging problems unsolved by existing employees. Good Hunting!

Additional Reading: Look for <u>The Resume Factory</u> by Lawrence Peterson, 2012, ISBN: 9781301515998 for examples of resumes shown to attract offers.

Back to Table of Contents